D0603952

100 Best HAMBURGER RECIPES

pil

Publications International, Ltd.
Favorite Brand Name Recipes at www.fbnr.com

Microwave Cooking: Microwave ovens vary in wattage. Use the cooking times as guidelines and check for doneness before adding more time.

Preparation/Cooking Times: Preparation times are based on the approximate amount of time required to assemble the recipe before cooking, baking, chilling or serving. These times include preparation steps such as measuring, chopping and mixing. The fact that some preparations and cooking can be done simultaneously is taken into account. Preparation of optional ingredients and serving suggestions is not included.

Contents

Hamburger
CLASSICS

Hearty Nachos

1 pound ground beef
1 envelope LIPTON® RECIPE SECRETS® Onion Soup Mix
1 can (19 ounces) black beans, rinsed and drained
1 cup prepared salsa
1 package (8½ ounces) plain tortilla chips
1 cup shredded Cheddar cheese (about 4 ounces)

1. In 12-inch nonstick skillet, brown ground beef over medium-high heat; drain.

2. Stir in soup mix, black beans and salsa. Bring to a boil over high heat. Reduce heat to low and simmer 5 minutes or until heated through.

3. Arrange tortilla chips on serving platter. Spread beef mixture over chips; sprinkle with Cheddar cheese. Top, if desired, with sliced green onions, sliced pitted ripe olives, chopped tomato and chopped cilantro.

Makes 8 servings

Prep Time: 10 minutes
Cook Time: 12 minutes

Hearty Nachos

Heartland Shepherd's Pie

¾ **pound ground beef**
1 **medium onion, chopped**
1 **can (14½ ounces) DEL MONTE® Original Recipe Stewed Tomatoes**
1 **can (8 ounces) DEL MONTE Tomato Sauce**
1 **can (14½ ounces) DEL MONTE Mixed Vegetables, drained**
   Instant mashed potato flakes plus ingredients to prepare (enough for 6 servings)
3 **cloves garlic, minced (optional)**

1. Preheat oven to 375°F. In large skillet, brown meat and onion over medium-high heat; drain.

2. Add tomatoes and tomato sauce; cook over high heat until thickened, stirring frequently. Stir in mixed vegetables. Season with salt and pepper, if desired.

3. Spoon into 2-quart baking dish; set aside. Prepare 6 servings mashed potatoes according to package directions, first cooking garlic in specified amount of butter.

4. Top meat mixture with potatoes. Bake 20 minutes or until heated through. Garnish with chopped parsley, if desired.

Makes 4 to 6 servings

Prep Time: 5 minutes
Cook Time: 30 minutes

Heartland Shepherd's Pie

Backyard Barbecue Burgers

1½ **pounds ground beef**
⅓ **cup barbecue sauce, divided**
1 **onion, peeled and sliced**
1 **to 2 tomatoes, sliced**
1 **to 2 tablespoons olive oil**
6 **kaiser rolls, split**
   Green or red leaf lettuce

1. Prepare grill for direct grilling. Combine ground beef and 2 tablespoons barbecue sauce in large bowl. Shape into six 1-inch-thick patties.

2. Place patties on grid directly above medium-hot coals. Grill, uncovered, until no longer pink in center (160°F), turning and brushing often with remaining barbecue sauce.

3. Meanwhile, brush onion and tomato slices with oil.* Place on grid. Grill onion slices about 10 minutes and tomato slices about 2 to 3 minutes.

4. Just before serving, place rolls, cut side down, on grid and grill until toasted. Serve patties on toasted rolls with grilled onions, tomatoes and lettuce.   *Makes 6 servings*

Onion slices may also be cooked in 2 tablespoons oil in large skillet over medium heat 10 minutes until tender and slightly brown.

Backyard Barbecue Burger

Southwestern Meat Loaf

1 envelope LIPTON® RECIPE SECRETS® Onion Soup Mix*
2 pounds ground beef
2 cups (about 3 ounces) cornflakes or bran flakes cereal, crushed
1½ cups frozen or drained canned whole kernel corn
1 small green bell pepper, chopped
2 eggs
¾ cup water
⅓ cup ketchup

*Also terrific with LIPTON® RECIPE SECRETS® Onion-Mushroom or Beefy Onion Soup Mix.

1. Preheat oven to 350°F. In large bowl, combine all ingredients.

2. In 13×9-inch baking or roasting pan, shape into loaf.

3. Bake uncovered 1 hour or until done. Let stand 10 minutes before serving. Serve, if desired, with salsa.   *Makes 8 servings*

Recipe Tip: For a great lunchbox treat, wrap leftover meat loaf slices in a tortilla and top with your favorite taco toppings such as salsa, sour cream, grated cheese and shredded lettuce.

Southwestern Meat Loaf

Chili-Stuffed Poblano Peppers

1 pound lean ground beef
4 large poblano peppers
1 can (15 ounces) chili-seasoned beans
1 can (14½ ounces) chili-style chunky tomatoes, undrained
1 tablespoon Mexican (Adobo) seasoning
⅔ cup shredded Mexican cheese blend or Monterey Jack cheese

1. Preheat broiler. Bring 2 quarts water to a boil in 3-quart saucepan. Cook ground beef in large nonstick skillet over medium-high heat 5 to 6 minutes or until no longer pink.

2. While meat is cooking, cut peppers in half lengthwise; remove stems and seeds. Add 4 pepper halves to boiling water; cook 3 minutes or until bright green and slightly softened. Remove; drain upside down on plate. Repeat with remaining 4 halves. Set aside.

3. Add beans, tomatoes and Mexican seasoning to ground beef. Cook and stir over medium heat 5 minutes or until mixture thickens slightly.

4. Arrange peppers, cut side up, in 13×9-inch baking dish. Divide chili mixture evenly among each pepper; top with cheese. Broil 6 inches from heat 1 minute or until cheese is melted. Serve immediately.

Makes 4 servings

Serving Suggestion: Serve with cornbread and chunky salsa.

Prep and Cook Time: 26 minutes

Chili-Stuffed Poblano Pepper

Old-Fashioned Beef Pot Pie

   1 pound ground beef
   1 can (11 ounces) condensed beef with vegetables and barley soup
 ½ cup water
   1 package (10 ounces) frozen peas and carrots, thawed and drained
 ½ teaspoon seasoned salt
 ⅛ teaspoon garlic powder
 ⅛ teaspoon ground black pepper
   1 cup (4 ounces) shredded Cheddar cheese, divided
1⅓ cups *French's*® French Fried Onions, divided
   1 package (7.5 ounces) refrigerated biscuits

Preheat oven to 350°F. In large skillet, brown ground beef in large chunks; drain. Stir in soup, water, vegetables and seasonings; bring to a boil. Reduce heat and simmer, uncovered, 5 minutes. Remove from heat; stir in ½ cup cheese and ⅔ *cup* French Fried Onions.

Pour mixture into 12×8-inch baking dish. Cut each biscuit in half; place, cut side down, around edge of casserole. Bake, uncovered, 15 to 20 minutes or until biscuits are done. Top with remaining cheese and ⅔ *cup* onions; bake, uncovered, 5 minutes or until onions are golden brown.   *Makes 4 to 6 servings*

Tip

Ground beef labels usually indicate the percentage of fat in the meat. If you don't see that number, look at the meat—meat that has more fat will be lighter in color than leaner meat.

Old-Fashioned Beef Pot Pie

Special Occasion Meat Loaf

 1 pound ground beef
 1 pound Italian sausage, removed from casings and crumbled
1½ cups seasoned bread crumbs
 2 eggs, lightly beaten
 2 tablespoons chopped fresh parsley
 2 cloves garlic, minced
 1 teaspoon salt
 ½ teaspoon black pepper
 2 cups water
 1 tablespoon butter
 1 package (about 4 ounces) Spanish rice mix
 2 packages (10 ounces each) frozen chopped spinach, thawed and
    well drained

Combine ground beef, sausage, bread crumbs, eggs, parsley, garlic, salt and pepper in large bowl; mix well. Place on 12×12-inch sheet of foil moistened with water. Cover with 12×14-inch sheet of waxed paper moistened with water. Press meat mixture into 12×12-inch rectangle with hands or rolling pin. Refrigerate 2 hours or until well chilled.

Bring water, butter and rice mix to a boil in medium saucepan. Continue boiling over medium heat 10 minutes or until rice is tender, stirring occasionally. Refrigerate 2 hours or until well chilled.

Preheat oven to 350°F. Remove waxed paper from ground beef mixture. Spread spinach over ground beef mixture, leaving 1-inch border. Spread rice evenly over spinach. Starting at long end, roll up jelly-roll style, using foil as a guide and removing foil after rolling. Seal edges tightly. Place meat loaf seam side down in 13×9-inch baking pan. Bake, uncovered, about 1 hour. Let stand 15 minutes before serving. Cut into 1-inch slices. *Makes about 8 servings*

Special Occasion Meat Loaf

Lipton® Onion Burgers

1 envelope LIPTON® RECIPE SECRETS® Onion Soup Mix*
2 pounds ground beef
½ cup water

*Also terrific with LIPTON® RECIPE SECRETS® Beefy Onion, Onion Mushroom, Beefy Mushroom, Savory Herb with Garlic or Ranch Soup Mix.

1. In large bowl, combine all ingredients; shape into 8 patties.

2. Grill or broil until done.   *Makes about 8 servings*

Prep Time: 10 minutes
Cook Time: 12 minutes

Kid's Choice Meatballs

1½ pounds ground beef
¼ cup dry seasoned bread crumbs
¼ cup grated Parmesan cheese
3 tablespoons *French's*® Worcestershire Sauce
1 egg
2 jars (14 ounces *each*) spaghetti sauce

1. Preheat oven to 425°F. In bowl, gently mix beef, bread crumbs, cheese, Worcestershire and egg. Shape into 1-inch meatballs. Place on rack in roasting pan. Bake 15 minutes or until cooked.

2. In large saucepan, combine meatballs and spaghetti sauce. Cook until heated through. Serve over cooked pasta.
                    Makes 6 to 8 servings (about 48 meatballs)

Quick Meatball Tip: On waxed paper, pat meat mixture into 8×6×1-inch rectangle. With knife, cut crosswise and lengthwise into 1-inch rows. Roll each small square into a ball.

Prep Time: 10 minutes
Cook Time: 20 minutes

Lipton® Onion Burgers

Lasagna Supreme

8 ounces uncooked lasagna noodles
½ pound ground beef
½ pound mild Italian sausage, casings removed
1 medium onion, chopped
2 cloves garlic, minced
1 can (14½ ounces) whole peeled tomatoes, undrained, chopped
1 can (6 ounces) tomato paste
2 teaspoons dried basil leaves
1 teaspoon dried marjoram leaves
1 can (4 ounces) sliced mushrooms, drained
2 eggs
2 cups (16 ounces) cream-style cottage cheese
¾ cup grated Parmesan cheese, divided
2 tablespoons dried parsley flakes
½ teaspoon salt
½ teaspoon black pepper
2 cups (8 ounces) shredded Cheddar cheese
3 cups (12 ounces) shredded mozzarella cheese

1. Cook lasagna noodles according to package directions; drain. Cook meats, onion and garlic in large skillet over medium-high heat until meat is brown, stirring to separate meat. Drain drippings.

2. Add tomatoes with juice, tomato paste, basil and marjoram. Reduce heat to low. Cover; simmer 15 minutes, stirring often. Stir in mushrooms; set aside.

3. Preheat oven to 375°F. Beat eggs in large bowl; add cottage cheese, ½ cup Parmesan cheese, parsley, salt and pepper. Mix well.

4. Place half the noodles in bottom of greased 13×9-inch baking pan. Spread half the cottage cheese mixture over noodles, then half the meat mixture and half the Cheddar cheese and mozzarella cheese. Repeat layers. Sprinkle with remaining ¼ cup Parmesan cheese.

5. Bake lasagna 40 to 45 minutes or until bubbly. Let stand 10 minutes before cutting. *Makes 8 to 10 servings*

Lasagna Supreme

Beefy Calzones

1 pound ground beef
¼ cup finely chopped onion
¼ cup finely chopped green bell pepper
2 cloves garlic, minced
1 (15-ounce) can tomato sauce
½ cup A.1.® THICK & HEARTY Steak Sauce
1 teaspoon Italian seasoning
2 (11-ounce) packages refrigerated pizza crust dough
2 cups shredded mozzarella cheese (8 ounces)

In large skillet, over medium-high heat, cook beef, onion, pepper and garlic until beef is no longer pink, stirring to break up meat; drain. Keep warm.

In small skillet, over medium-high heat, heat tomato sauce, steak sauce and Italian seasoning to a boil. Reduce heat to low; simmer 5 minutes or until slightly thickened. Stir 1 cup tomato sauce mixture into beef mixture; set aside. Keep remaining tomato sauce mixture warm.

Unroll pizza dough from 1 package; divide into 4 equal pieces. Roll each piece into 6-inch square; spoon ⅓ cup reserved beef mixture onto center of each square. Top with ¼ cup cheese. Fold dough over to form triangle. Press edges together, sealing well with tines of fork. Place on lightly greased baking sheets. Repeat with remaining dough, filling and cheese to make a total of 8 calzones. Bake at 400°F 20 minutes or until golden brown. Serve with warm sauce. Garnish as desired.

Makes 8 servings

Beefy Calzones

Original Ortega® Taco Recipe

1 pound ground beef
¾ cup water
1 package (1¼ ounces) ORTEGA® Taco Seasoning Mix
1 package (12) ORTEGA® Taco Shells, warmed
   Toppings: shredded lettuce, chopped tomatoes, shredded mild
      Cheddar cheese, ORTEGA® Thick & Smooth Taco Sauce

BROWN beef; drain. Stir in water and seasoning mix. Bring to a boil. Reduce heat to low; cook, stirring occasionally, for 5 to 6 minutes or until mixture is thickened.

FILL taco shells with beef mixture. Top with lettuce, tomatoes, cheese and taco sauce. *Makes 6 servings*

Classic Hamburger Casserole

1 pound ground beef
1 package (9 ounces) frozen cut green beans, thawed and drained
1 can (10¾ ounces) condensed tomato soup
¼ cup water
½ teaspoon seasoned salt
⅛ teaspoon pepper
2 cups hot mashed potatoes
1⅓ cups *French's*® French Fried Onions, divided
½ cup (2 ounces) shredded Cheddar cheese

Preheat oven to 350°F. In medium skillet, brown ground beef; drain. Stir in green beans, soup, water and seasonings; pour into 1½-quart casserole. In medium bowl, combine mashed potatoes and ⅔ *cup* French Fried Onions. Spoon potato mixture in mounds around edge of casserole. Bake, uncovered, at 350°F for 25 minutes or until heated through. Top potatoes with cheese and remaining ⅔ *cup* onions; bake, uncovered, 5 minutes or until onions are golden brown.
Makes 4 to 6 servings

Original Ortega® Taco Recipe

Mama's Best Ever Spaghetti & Meatballs

1 pound lean ground beef
½ cup Italian seasoned dry bread crumbs
1 egg
1 jar (26 to 28 ounces) RAGÚ® Old World Style® Pasta Sauce
8 ounces spaghetti, cooked and drained

1. In medium bowl, combine ground beef, bread crumbs and egg; shape into 12 meatballs.

2. In 3-quart saucepan, bring Ragú Pasta Sauce to a boil over medium-high heat. Gently stir in meatballs.

3. Reduce heat to low and simmer covered, stirring occasionally, 20 minutes or until meatballs are no longer pink in centers. Serve over hot spaghetti; sprinkle with shredded Parmesan cheese if desired.

Makes 4 servings

Prep Time: 10 minutes
Cook Time: 20 minutes

Pizza Meat Loaf

1 envelope LIPTON® RECIPE SECRETS® Onion Soup Mix*
2 pounds ground beef
1½ cups fresh bread crumbs
2 eggs
1 small green bell pepper, chopped (optional)
¼ cup water
1 cup RAGÚ® OLD WORLD STYLE® Pasta Sauce, divided
1 cup shredded mozzarella cheese (about 4 ounces), divided

*Also terrific with LIPTON® RECIPE SECRETS® Savory Herb with Garlic Soup Mix.

1. Preheat oven to 350°F. In large bowl, combine all ingredients except ½ cup pasta sauce and ½ cup cheese.

2. In 13×9-inch baking or roasting pan, shape into loaf. Top with remaining ½ cup pasta sauce.

3. Bake uncovered 50 minutes.

4. Sprinkle top with remaining ½ cup cheese. Bake an additional 10 minutes or until done. Let stand 10 minutes before serving.

Makes 8 servings

Recipe Tip: When grating cheese, spray your box grater with nonstick cooking spray and place on a sheet of waxed paper. When you finish grating, clean-up is a breeze. Simply discard the waxed paper and rinse the grater clean.

Pizza Meat Loaf

Mediterranean Burgers

½ **cup feta cheese (2 ounces)**
¼ **cup A.1.® Original or A.1.® BOLD & SPICY Steak Sauce, divided**
2 **tablespoons sliced pitted ripe olives**
2 **tablespoons mayonnaise**
1 **pound ground beef**
4 **(5-inch) pita breads**
4 **radicchio leaves**
4 **tomato slices**

Mix feta cheese, 2 tablespoons steak sauce, olives and mayonnaise.
Cover; refrigerate at least one hour or up to 2 days.

Shape beef into 4 patties. Grill burgers over medium heat or broil
6 inches from heat source 5 minutes on each side or until no longer
pink in center, basting with remaining 2 tablespoons steak sauce.

Split open top edge of each pita bread. Arrange 1 radicchio
leaf in each pita pocket; top each with burger, tomato slice
and 2 tablespoons chilled sauce. Serve immediately.

Makes 4 burgers

Mediterranean Burger

Aztec Chili Salad

   1 pound ground beef
   1 package (1.48 ounces) LAWRY'S® Spices & Seasonings for Chili
   ½ cup water
   1 can (15¼ ounces) kidney beans, undrained
   1 can (14½ ounces) whole peeled tomatoes, cut up, undrained
   ½ cup sour cream
   3 tablespoons mayonnaise
   1 fresh medium tomato, diced
   ¼ cup chopped fresh cilantro
   ½ teaspoon LAWRY'S® Seasoned Pepper
   1 head lettuce
   1 red bell pepper, sliced
   ¼ cup sliced green onions
 1½ cups (6 ounces) shredded cheddar cheese
   ¼ cup sliced ripe olives

In large skillet, cook ground beef over medium-high heat until crumbly; drain fat. Add Spices & Seasonings for Chili, water, beans and canned tomatoes; mix well. Bring to a boil over medium-high heat; reduce heat to low and simmer, uncovered, 10 minutes. For dressing, in blender or food processor, blend sour cream, mayonnaise, fresh tomato, cilantro and Seasoned Pepper. Refrigerate until chilled. On 6 individual plates, layer lettuce, chili meat, bell pepper, onions, cheese and olives. Drizzle with chilled dressing.   *Makes 6 servings*

Serving Suggestion: Excellent with tortillas or corn muffins.

Aztec Chili Salad

Zesty Italian Stuffed Peppers

3 bell peppers (green, red or yellow)
1 pound ground beef
1 jar (14 ounces) spaghetti sauce
1⅓ cups *French's®* **French Fried Onions, divided**
2 tablespoons *Frank's®* **RedHot® Cayenne Pepper Sauce**
½ cup uncooked instant rice
¼ cup sliced ripe olives
1 cup (4 ounces) shredded mozzarella cheese

Preheat oven to 400°F. Cut bell peppers in half lengthwise through stems; discard seeds. Place pepper halves, cut side up, in 2-quart shallow baking dish; set aside.

Place beef in large microwavable bowl. Microwave on HIGH 5 minutes or until meat is browned, stirring once. Drain. Stir in spaghetti sauce, ⅔ *cup* French Fried Onions, **Frank's RedHot** Sauce, rice and olives. Spoon evenly into bell pepper halves.

Cover; bake 35 minutes or until bell peppers are tender. Uncover; sprinkle with cheese and remaining ⅔ *cup* onions. Bake 1 minute or until onions are golden. *Makes 6 servings*

Prep Time: 10 minutes
Cook Time: 36 minutes

Zesty Italian Stuffed Pepper

Beef Stroganoff Casserole

 1 pound lean ground beef
 ¼ teaspoon salt
 ⅛ teaspoon black pepper
 1 teaspoon vegetable oil
 8 ounces sliced mushrooms
 1 large onion, chopped
 3 cloves garlic, minced
 ¼ cup dry white wine
 1 can (10¾ ounces) condensed cream of mushroom soup, undiluted
 ½ cup sour cream
 1 tablespoon Dijon mustard
 4 cups cooked egg noodles
   Chopped fresh parsley (optional)

Preheat oven to 350°F. Spray 13×9-inch baking dish with nonstick cooking spray.

Place beef in large skillet; season with salt and pepper. Brown beef over medium-high heat until no longer pink, stirring to separate beef. Drain fat from skillet; set beef aside.

Heat oil in same skillet over medium-high heat until hot. Add mushrooms, onion and garlic; cook and stir 2 minutes or until onion is tender. Add wine. Reduce heat to medium-low and simmer 3 minutes. Remove from heat; stir in soup, sour cream and mustard until well combined. Return beef to skillet.

Place noodles in prepared dish. Pour beef mixture over noodles; stir until noodles are well coated.

Bake, uncovered, 30 minutes or until heated through. Sprinkle with parsley, if desired.

Makes 6 servings

Beef Stroganoff Casserole

Roasted Garlic Swedish Meatballs

1 pound ground beef
½ cup plain dry bread crumbs
1 egg
1 jar (16 ounces) RAGÚ® Cheese Creations!® Roasted Garlic Parmesan Sauce
1¼ cups beef broth
2 teaspoons Worcestershire sauce
1 teaspoon ground allspice (optional)

In large bowl, combine ground beef, bread crumbs and egg; shape into 20 (1½-inch) meatballs.

In 12-inch nonstick skillet, brown meatballs over medium-high heat.

Meanwhile, in medium bowl, combine Ragú Cheese Creations! Sauce, beef broth, Worcestershire sauce and allspice; stir into skillet. Bring to a boil over high heat. Reduce heat to low and simmer uncovered, stirring occasionally, 10 minutes or until meatballs are done and sauce is slightly thickened. Serve, if desired, over hot cooked noodles or rice.

Makes 4 servings

Tip

Allspice, used in both sweet and savory dishes, tastes like a combination of cinnamon, nutmeg and cloves. Like other spices, it should be purchased in small amounts and stored in a cool, dark place for up to six months.

Roasted Garlic Swedish Meatballs

Souperior Meat Loaf

   2 pounds ground beef
   ¾ cup plain dry bread crumbs*
   1 envelope LIPTON® RECIPE SECRETS® Onion Soup Mix**
   ¾ cup water
   ⅓ cup ketchup
   2 eggs

Substitution: Use 1½ cups fresh bread crumbs or 5 slices fresh bread, cubed.

**Also terrific with LIPTON® RECIPE SECRETS® Beefy Onion, Onion Mushroom, Beefy Mushroom or Savory Herb with Garlic Soup Mix.*

1. Preheat oven to 350°F. In large bowl, combine all ingredients.

2. In 13×9-inch baking or roasting pan, shape into loaf.

3. Bake uncovered 1 hour or until done. Let stand 10 minutes before serving.   *Makes 8 servings*

Slow Cooker Method: Place meat loaf in slow cooker. Cover. Cook on HIGH for 4 hours or LOW 6 to 8 hours.

Helpful Hint: Placing meat loaf on a piece of cheesecloth and then on a rack helps to hold the meat together while lifting in and out of slow cooker.

Recipe Tip: It's a snap to make fresh bread crumbs. Simply process fresh or day old white, Italian or French bread in a food processor or blender until fine crumbs form.

Prep Time: 10 minutes
Cook Time: 1 hour

Souperior Meat Loaf

America's Favorite Cheddar Beef Burgers

1 pound ground beef
⅓ cup A.1.® Steak Sauce, divided
1 medium onion, cut into strips
1 medium green or red bell pepper, cut into strips
1 tablespoon margarine or butter
4 ounces Cheddar cheese, sliced
4 hamburger rolls
4 tomato slices

Mix ground beef and 3 tablespoons steak sauce; shape mixture into 4 burgers. Set aside.

Cook and stir onion and pepper in margarine or butter in medium skillet until tender. Stir in remaining steak sauce; keep warm.

Grill burgers over medium heat for 4 minutes on each side or until done. When almost done, top with cheese; grill until cheese melts. Spoon 2 tablespoons onion mixture onto each roll bottom; top each with burger, tomato slice, some of remaining onion mixture and roll top. Serve immediately.   *Makes 4 servings*

America's Favorite Cheddar Beef Burger

Beefy Nacho Crescent Bake

1 pound lean ground beef
½ cup chopped onion
¼ teaspoon salt
⅛ teaspoon black pepper
1 tablespoon chili powder
1 teaspoon ground cumin
1 teaspoon dried oregano leaves
1 can (11 ounces) condensed nacho cheese soup, undiluted
1 cup milk
1 can (8 ounces) refrigerated crescent roll dough
¼ cup (1 ounce) shredded Cheddar cheese
   Chopped fresh cilantro (optional)
   Salsa (optional)

Preheat oven to 375°F. Spray 13×9-inch baking dish with nonstick cooking spray.

Place beef and onion in large skillet; season with salt and pepper. Brown beef over medium-high heat until no longer pink, stirring to separate meat. Drain fat. Stir in chili powder, cumin and oregano. Cook and stir 2 minutes; remove from heat.

Combine soup and milk in medium bowl, stirring until smooth. Pour soup mixture into prepared dish, spreading evenly.

Separate crescent dough into 4 rectangles; press perforations together firmly. Roll each rectangle to 8×4 inches. Cut each rectangle in half crosswise to form 8 (4-inch) squares.

Spoon about ¼ cup beef mixture in center of each square. Lift 4 corners of dough up over filling to meet in center; pinch and twist firmly to seal. Place squares in dish.

Bake, uncovered, 20 to 25 minutes or until crusts are golden brown. Sprinkle cheese over squares. Bake 5 minutes or until cheese melts. To serve, spoon soup mixture in dish over each serving; sprinkle with cilantro, if desired. Serve with salsa, if desired.   *Makes 4 servings*

Beefy Nacho Crescent Bake

Hamburger Classics

Contadina® Classic Lasagne

1 pound dry lasagne noodles, cooked
1 tablespoon olive or vegetable oil
1 cup chopped onion
½ cup chopped green bell pepper
2 cloves garlic, minced
1½ pounds lean ground beef
2 cans (14.5 ounces each) CONTADINA® Recipe Ready Diced Tomatoes, undrained
1 can (8 ounces) CONTADINA® Tomato Sauce
1 can (6 ounces) CONTADINA® Tomato Paste
½ cup dry red wine or beef broth
1½ teaspoons salt
1 teaspoon dried oregano leaves, crushed
1 teaspoon dried basil leaves, crushed
½ teaspoon ground black pepper
1 egg
1 cup (8 ounces) ricotta cheese
2 cups (8 ounces) shredded mozzarella cheese, divided

1. Cook pasta according to package directions; drain. Meanwhile, heat oil in large skillet. Add onion, bell pepper and garlic; sauté for 3 minutes or until vegetables are tender. Add beef; cook for 5 to 6 minutes or until evenly browned.

2. Add tomatoes and juice, tomato sauce, tomato paste, wine, salt, oregano, basil and black pepper; bring to a boil. Reduce heat to low; simmer, uncovered, for 20 minutes, stirring occasionally.

3. Beat egg slightly in medium bowl. Stir in ricotta cheese and 1 cup mozzarella cheese.

4. Layer noodles, half of meat sauce, noodles, all of ricotta cheese mixture, noodles and remaining meat sauce in ungreased 13×9-inch baking dish. Sprinkle with remaining mozzarella cheese.

5. Bake in preheated 350°F oven for 25 to 30 minutes or until heated through. Let stand 10 minutes before cutting.   *Makes 10 servings*

Contadina® Classic Lasagne

Suzie's Sloppy Joes

 3 pounds lean ground beef
 1 cup chopped onion
 3 cloves garlic, minced
1¼ cups ketchup
 1 cup chopped red bell pepper
 5 tablespoons Worcestershire sauce
 4 tablespoons brown sugar
 3 tablespoons vinegar
 3 tablespoons prepared mustard
 2 teaspoons chili powder
   Hamburger buns

SLOW COOKER DIRECTIONS
Brown ground beef, onion and garlic in large skillet. Drain excess fat.

Combine ketchup, bell pepper, Worcestershire sauce, brown sugar, vinegar, mustard and chili powder in slow cooker. Stir in beef mixture. Cover and cook on LOW 6 to 8 hours. Spoon into hamburger buns.

Makes 8 to 10 servings

Tip There are many choices of ground beef in the supermarket; the names indicate the cut of meat that was ground. The leanest of these is ground sirloin, which contains about 15 percent fat, followed by ground round, with 20 to 23 percent fat, and ground chuck at 23 to 30 percent fat.

Suzie's Sloppy Joes

Mexican Taco Salad

1 pound ground beef or turkey
1 cup (1 small) chopped onion
1 cup ORTEGA® Salsa Prima-Thick & Chunky Mild
¾ cup water
1 package (1¼ ounces) ORTEGA® Taco Seasoning Mix
1¾ cups (15-ounce can) kidney or pinto beans, rinsed and drained
½ cup (4-ounce can) ORTEGA® Diced Green Chiles
6 tortilla shells or 3 cups (3 ounces) tortilla chips
6 cups shredded lettuce, *divided*
  Chopped tomatoes (optional)
¾ cup (3 ounces) shredded Nacho & Taco blend cheese, *divided*
  Sour cream (optional)
  Guacamole (optional)
  ORTEGA® Thick & Smooth Taco Sauce

COOK beef and onion until beef is brown; drain. Stir in salsa, water and seasoning mix. Bring to a boil. Reduce heat to low; cook for 2 to 3 minutes. Stir in beans and chiles.

LAYER ingredients as follows in *each* shell: *1 cup* lettuce, *¾ cup* meat mixture, tomatoes, *2 tablespoons* cheese and sour cream. Serve with guacamole and taco sauce.   *Makes 6 servings*

Mexican Taco Salad

Dijon Bacon Cheeseburgers

1 cup shredded Cheddar cheese (4 ounces)
5 tablespoons GREY POUPON® Dijon Mustard, divided
2 teaspoons dried minced onion
1 teaspoon prepared horseradish
1 pound lean ground beef
4 onion sandwich rolls, split and toasted
1 cup shredded lettuce
4 slices tomato
4 slices bacon, cooked and halved

In small bowl, combine cheese, 3 tablespoons mustard, onion and horseradish; set aside.

In medium bowl, combine ground beef and remaining mustard; shape mixture into 4 patties. Grill or broil burgers over medium heat for 5 minutes on each side or until desired doneness; top with cheese mixture and cook until cheese melts, about 2 minutes. Top each roll bottom with ¼ cup shredded lettuce, 1 tomato slice, burger, 2 bacon pieces and roll top. Serve immediately. *Makes 4 burgers*

Dijon Bacon Cheeseburger

Casseroles

String Pie

- **1 pound ground beef**
- **½ cup chopped onion**
- **¼ cup chopped green pepper**
- **1 jar (15½ ounces) spaghetti sauce**
- **8 ounces spaghetti, cooked and drained**
- **⅓ cup grated Parmesan cheese**
- **2 eggs, beaten**
- **2 teaspoons butter**
- **1 cup cottage cheese**
- **½ cup (2 ounces) shredded mozzarella cheese**

Preheat oven to 350°F. Cook beef, onion and green pepper in large skillet over medium-high heat until meat is browned. Drain fat. Stir in spaghetti sauce. Combine spaghetti, Parmesan cheese, eggs and butter in large bowl; mix well. Place in bottom of 13×9-inch baking pan. Spread cottage cheese over top; cover with sauce mixture. Sprinkle with mozzarella cheese. Bake until mixture is thoroughly heated and cheese is melted, about 20 minutes.

Makes 6 to 8 servings

*Favorite recipe from **North Dakota Beef Commission***

String Pie

Stuffed Mushrooms with Pasta

1 pound extra-lean (90% lean) ground beef
¼ cup finely chopped onion
¼ cup finely chopped green or red bell pepper
1 large clove garlic, minced
2 tablespoons finely chopped fresh parsley
2 teaspoons finely chopped fresh basil *or* 1 teaspoon dried basil leaves, crushed
1 teaspoon finely chopped fresh oregano *or* ½ teaspoon dried oregano leaves, crushed
½ teaspoon salt
   Dash black pepper
12 very large mushrooms
3 cups prepared spaghetti sauce
¼ cup (1 ounce) grated Parmesan cheese
4½ cups cooked spaghetti

Preheat oven to 350°F.

Combine ground beef, onion, green bell pepper, garlic, parsley, basil, oregano, salt and black pepper in medium bowl; mix lightly. Remove stems from mushrooms; finely chop stems. Add to ground beef mixture. Stuff into mushroom caps, rounding tops.

Pour spaghetti sauce into shallow casserole dish large enough to hold mushrooms in single layer. Place mushrooms, stuffing side up, in sauce; cover.

Bake 20 minutes; remove cover. Sprinkle with Parmesan cheese. Continue baking, uncovered, 15 minutes. Serve with spaghetti. Garnish with additional fresh basil leaves, if desired.

Makes 6 servings

Stuffed Mushrooms with Pasta

Layered Mexican Casserole

8 ounces ground beef
1 (12-ounce) can whole kernel corn, drained
1 (12-ounce) jar chunky salsa
1 (2¼-ounce) can sliced pitted ripe olives, drained
1 cup cream-style cottage cheese
1 (8-ounce) carton dairy sour cream
5 cups tortilla chips (7 to 8 ounces)
2 cups (8 ounces) shredded Wisconsin Cheddar cheese, divided
½ cup chopped tomato

Brown ground beef in large skillet; drain. Add corn and salsa; cook until thoroughly heated. Reserve 2 tablespoons olives; stir remaining olives into beef mixture. Combine cottage cheese and sour cream in bowl.

In 2-quart casserole, layer 2 cups chips, half of meat mixture, ¾ cup Cheddar cheese and half of cottage cheese mixture. Repeat layers; cover. Bake in preheated 350°F oven 35 minutes. Line edge of casserole with remaining 1 cup chips; top with tomato, reserved 2 tablespoons olives and remaining ½ cup Cheddar cheese. Bake 10 minutes or until cheese is melted and chips are hot.

Makes 4 to 6 servings

*Favorite recipe from **Wisconsin Milk Marketing Board***

Layered Mexican Casserole

Shepherd's Pie

1⅓ cups instant mashed potato buds
1⅔ cups milk
2 tablespoons margarine or butter
1 teaspoon salt, divided
1 pound ground beef
¼ teaspoon black pepper
1 jar (12 ounces) beef gravy
1 package (10 ounces) frozen mixed vegetables, thawed and drained
¾ cup grated Parmesan cheese

1. Preheat broiler. Prepare 4 servings of mashed potatoes according to package directions using milk, margarine and ½ teaspoon salt.

2. While mashed potatoes are cooking, brown meat in medium broilerproof skillet over medium-high heat, stirring to separate meat. Drain drippings. Sprinkle meat with remaining ½ teaspoon salt and pepper. Add gravy and vegetables; mix well. Cook over medium-low heat 5 minutes or until hot.

3. Spoon prepared potatoes around outside edge of skillet, leaving 3-inch circle in center. Sprinkle cheese evenly over potatoes. Broil 4 to 5 inches from heat source 3 minutes or until cheese is golden brown and meat mixture is bubbly.   *Makes 4 servings*

Prep and Cook Time: 28 minutes

Shepherd's Pie

Tamale Beef Squares

1 (6½-ounce) package corn muffin and cornbread mix
⅓ cup fat-free (skim) milk
¼ cup cholesterol-free egg substitute
1 tablespoon canola oil
1 pound lean ground beef
¾ cup chopped onion
1 cup frozen corn kernels
1 (14½-ounce) can Mexican-style stewed tomatoes, undrained
2 teaspoons cornstarch
¾ cup shredded reduced-fat sharp Cheddar cheese (3 ounces)

1. Preheat oven to 400°F. Spray 12×8-inch baking dish with nonstick cooking spray.

2. Stir together corn muffin mix, milk, egg substitute and oil. Spread in bottom of prepared dish.

3. Cook ground beef and onion in large skillet over medium-high heat until beef is lightly browned, stirring to break up meat; drain fat. Stir in corn.

4. Mix together undrained tomatoes and cornstarch, breaking up any large pieces of tomato. Stir into beef mixture. Bring to a boil, stirring frequently.

5. Spoon beef mixture over cornbread mixture. Cover with foil. Bake 15 minutes. Uncover; bake 10 minutes more. Sprinkle with cheese. Return to oven; bake 2 to 3 minutes or until cheese melts. Let stand 5 minutes. Cut into squares. *Makes 6 servings*

Tamale Beef Squares

Mexican Lasagna

**1 package (16 sheets) BARILLA® Oven Ready Lasagna Noodles
(do not boil)**
1 pound ground beef
1 package (1.5 ounces) taco seasoning
**1 jar (26 ounces) BARILLA® Lasagna & Casserole Sauce or Marinara
Pasta Sauce**
2 eggs
1 container (15 ounces) ricotta cheese
4 cups (16 ounces) shredded Mexican-style cheese, divided

1. Preheat oven to 375°F. Spray 13×9×2-inch baking pan with
nonstick cooking spray. Remove 12 lasagna noodles from package.
Do not boil.

2. Cook ground beef and taco seasoning in large skillet, following
directions on seasoning package. Remove from heat; stir in lasagna
sauce.

3. Beat eggs in medium bowl. Stir in ricotta cheese and 2 cups
Mexican-style cheese.

4. To assemble lasagna, spread 1 cup meat mixture over bottom
of pan. Arrange 4 uncooked lasagna noodles over meat mixture,
overlapping edges if necessary to fit pan. Top with half of ricotta
mixture and 1 cup meat mixture. Repeat layers (4 uncooked lasagna
noodles, remaining half of ricotta mixture and 1 cup meat mixture);
top with remaining 4 uncooked lasagna noodles, remaining meat
mixture and remaining 2 cups Mexican-style cheese.

5. Cover with foil and bake 45 to 55 minutes or until bubbly. Uncover
and continue cooking about 5 minutes or until cheese is melted. Let
stand 15 minutes before cutting.   *Makes 12 servings*

Mexican Lasagna

Artichoke Casserole

¾ **pound extra-lean (90% lean) ground beef**
½ **cup sliced mushrooms**
¼ **cup chopped onion**
 1 **clove garlic, minced**
 1 **can (14 ounces) artichoke hearts, drained, rinsed and chopped**
½ **cup dry bread crumbs**
¼ **cup (1 ounce) grated Parmesan cheese**
 2 **tablespoons chopped fresh rosemary** *or* **1 teaspoon dried rosemary**
1½ **teaspoons chopped fresh marjoram** *or* **½ teaspoon dried marjoram leaves**
   Salt and black pepper
 3 **egg whites**

Preheat oven to 400°F. Spray 1-quart casserole with nonstick cooking spray.

Brown ground beef in medium skillet. Drain. Add mushrooms, onion and garlic; cook until tender.

Combine ground beef mixture, artichokes, crumbs, cheese, rosemary and marjoram; mix lightly. Season with salt and pepper to taste.

Beat egg whites until stiff peaks form; fold into ground beef mixture. Spoon into prepared casserole.

Bake 20 minutes or until lightly browned around edges.

Makes 4 servings

Tortellini Bake Parmesano

1 package (12 ounces) fresh or frozen cheese tortellini or ravioli
½ pound lean ground beef
½ medium onion, finely chopped
2 cloves garlic, minced
½ teaspoon dried oregano, crushed
1 can (26 ounces) DEL MONTE® Chunky Spaghetti Sauce with Garlic & Herb
2 small zucchini, sliced
⅓ cup (about 1½ ounces) grated Parmesan cheese

1. Cook pasta according to package directions; rinse and drain.

2. Meanwhile, brown beef with onion, garlic and oregano in large skillet over medium-high heat; drain. Season with salt and pepper, if desired.

3. Add spaghetti sauce and zucchini. Cook 15 minutes or until thickened, stirring occasionally.

4. Arrange half of pasta in oiled 2-quart microwavable dish; top with half each of sauce and cheese. Repeat layers ending with cheese; cover.

5. Microwave on HIGH 8 to 10 minutes or until heated through, rotating dish halfway through cooking time.   *Makes 4 servings*

Hint: For convenience, double recipe and freeze one for later use. The recipe can also be made ahead, refrigerated and heated just before serving (allow extra time in microwave if dish is chilled).

Prep and Cook Time: 35 minutes

Italian-Style Meat Loaf

1 egg
1½ pounds lean ground beef or turkey
8 ounces hot or mild Italian sausage, casings removed
1 cup CONTADINA® Seasoned Bread Crumbs
1 can (8 ounces) CONTADINA Tomato Sauce, divided
1 cup finely chopped onion
½ cup finely chopped green bell pepper

1. Beat egg lightly in large bowl. Add beef, sausage, bread crumbs, ¾ cup tomato sauce, onion and bell pepper; mix well.

2. Press into ungreased 9×5-inch loaf pan. Bake, uncovered, in preheated 350°F oven for 60 minutes.

3. Spoon remaining tomato sauce over meat loaf. Bake 15 minutes longer or until no longer pink in center; drain. Let stand for 10 minutes before serving.   *Makes 8 servings*

Prep Time: 10 minutes
Cook Time: 75 minutes
Standing Time: 10 minutes

Italian-Style Meat Loaf

Moussaka

1 large eggplant, cut lengthwise into ½-inch-thick slices
2½ teaspoons salt, divided
½ cup olive oil, divided
2 russet potatoes, peeled, cut lengthwise into ¼-inch-thick slices
2 large zucchini, cut lengthwise into ⅜-inch-thick slices
1½ pounds ground beef or lamb
1 large onion, chopped
2 cloves garlic, minced
1 cup chopped tomatoes
½ cup dry red or white wine
¼ cup chopped fresh parsley
⅛ teaspoon *each* ground cinnamon and black pepper
1 cup grated Parmesan cheese, divided
4 tablespoons butter or margarine, divided
⅓ cup all-purpose flour
¼ teaspoon ground nutmeg
2 cups milk

Place eggplant in colander; sprinkle with 1 teaspoon salt. Drain 30 minutes. Heat ¼ cup oil in skillet over medium heat. Add potatoes in single layer. Cook 5 minutes per side or until tender. Drain on paper towels. Add more oil to skillet, if needed. Cook zucchini 2 minutes per side. Drain on paper towels. Add more oil to skillet. Cook eggplant 5 minutes per side. Drain on paper towels. Drain and discard oil. Heat skillet over medium-high heat until hot. Add beef, onion and garlic; cook and stir 5 minutes or until meat is no longer pink. Pour off drippings. Stir in tomatoes, wine, parsley, 1 teaspoon salt, cinnamon and pepper. Bring to a boil. Reduce heat to low; simmer 10 minutes or until liquid evaporates. Preheat oven to 325°F. Grease 13×9-inch baking dish. Layer potatoes, ¼ cup cheese, zucchini, ¼ cup cheese, eggplant and ¼ cup cheese. Top with meat mixture. Melt butter in saucepan over low heat. Whisk in flour, ½ teaspoon salt and nutmeg. Cook 1 minute, whisking constantly. Gradually whisk in milk. Whisk over medium heat until mixture boils and thickens. Pour mixture over meat mixture in dish; sprinkle with remaining ¼ cup cheese. Bake 30 to 40 minutes or until hot and bubbly.   *Makes 6 to 8 servings*

Moussaka

Quick Tamale Casserole

1½ pounds ground beef
¾ cup sliced green onions
1 can (4 ounces) chopped green chilies, drained and divided
1 can (10¾ ounces) condensed tomato soup
¾ cup salsa
1 can (16 ounces) whole kernel corn, drained
1 can (2¼ ounces) chopped pitted ripe olives (optional)
1 tablespoon Worcestershire sauce
1 teaspoon chili powder
¼ teaspoon garlic powder
4 slices (¾ ounce each) American cheese, halved
4 corn muffins, cut into ½-inch cubes
Mexican Sour Cream Topping (recipe follows, optional)

In medium skillet, brown ground beef with green onions. Reserve 2 tablespoons chilies for Mexican Sour Cream Topping, if desired. Stir in remaining chilies, tomato soup, salsa, corn, olives, Worcestershire sauce, chili powder and garlic powder until well blended. Place in 2-quart casserole. Top with cheese, then evenly spread muffin cubes over cheese. Bake at 350°F for 5 to 10 minutes or until cheese is melted. Serve with Mexican Sour Cream Topping, if desired.

Makes 6 servings

Mexican Sour Cream Topping

1 cup sour cream
2 tablespoons chopped green chilies, reserved from above
2 teaspoons chopped jalapeño peppers* (optional)
2 teaspoons lime juice

Jalapeño peppers can sting and irritate the skin; wear rubber gloves when handling peppers and do not touch eyes. Wash hands after handling.

Combine all ingredients in small bowl; mix until well blended.

Makes about 1 cup

Quick Tamale Casserole

Main-Dish Pie

1 package (8 rolls) refrigerated crescent rolls
1 pound lean ground beef
1 medium onion, chopped
1 can (12 ounces) beef or mushroom gravy
1 box (10 ounces) BIRDS EYE® frozen Green Peas, thawed
½ cup shredded Swiss cheese
6 slices tomato

• Preheat oven to 350°F.

• Unroll dough and separate rolls. Spread to cover bottom of ungreased 9-inch pie pan. Press together to form lower crust. Bake 10 minutes.

• Meanwhile, in large skillet, brown beef and onion; drain excess fat.

• Stir in gravy and peas; cook until heated through.

• Pour mixture into partially baked crust. Sprinkle with cheese.

• Bake 10 to 15 minutes or until crust is brown and cheese is melted.

• Arrange tomato slices over pie; bake 2 minutes more.

Makes 6 servings

Prep Time: 10 minutes
Cook Time: 20 to 25 minutes

Main-Dish Pie

Stuffed Mexican Pizza Pie

1 pound ground beef
1 large onion, chopped
1 large green bell pepper, chopped
1½ cups UNCLE BEN'S® Instant Rice
  2 cans (14½ ounces each) Mexican-style stewed tomatoes, undrained
⅔ cup water
  2 cups (8 ounces) shredded Mexican-style seasoned Monterey Jack-Colby cheese blend, divided
1 container (10 ounces) refrigerated pizza crust dough

1. Preheat oven to 425°F. Spray 13×9-inch baking pan with cooking spray; set aside.

2. Spray large nonstick skillet with nonstick cooking spray; heat over high heat until hot. Add beef, onion and bell pepper; cook and stir 5 minutes or until meat is no longer pink.

3. Add rice, stewed tomatoes and water. Bring to a boil. Pour beef mixture into prepared baking pan. Sprinkle with 1¼ cups cheese and stir until blended.

4. Unroll pizza crust dough on work surface. Place dough in one even layer over mixture in baking pan. Cut 6 to 8 slits in dough with sharp knife. Bake 10 minutes or until crust is lightly browned. Sprinkle top of crust with remaining ¾ cup cheese; continue baking 4 minutes or until cheese is melted and crust is deep golden brown.

5. Let stand 5 minutes before cutting. *Makes 6 servings*

Stuffed Mexican Pizza Pie

Ranch Lentil Casserole

2 cups lentils, rinsed
4 cups water
1 pound lean ground beef
1 cup water
1 cup ketchup
1 envelope dry onion soup mix
1 teaspoon prepared mustard
1 teaspoon vinegar

Cook lentils in 4 cups water for 30 minutes. Drain. Brown ground beef. Combine lentils, beef, 1 cup water and remaining ingredients in baking dish. Bake at 400°F for 30 minutes. *Makes 8 servings*

Note: Prepared recipe can be frozen.

Favorite recipe from **USA Dry Pea & Lentil Council**

Italian Pasta Bake

1 pound ground beef *or* Italian sausage
4 cups cooked mostaccioli *or* penne pasta
1 jar (28 to 30 ounces) spaghetti sauce (about 2¾ cups)
¾ cup KRAFT® 100% Grated Parmesan Cheese, divided
2 cups KRAFT® Shredded Low-Moisture Part-Skim Mozzarella Cheese

BROWN meat in large skillet; drain.

STIR in mostaccioli, spaghetti sauce and ½ cup of the Parmesan cheese. Spoon into 13×9-inch baking dish. Top with mozzarella cheese and remaining ¼ cup Parmesan cheese.

BAKE at 375°F for 20 minutes. *Makes 6 servings*

Prep Time: 10 minutes
Bake Time: 20 minutes

Family Favorite Hamburger Casserole

1 tablespoon CRISCO® Oil* plus additional for oiling
1 cup chopped onion
1 pound ground beef round
1 package (9 ounces) frozen cut green beans
3 cups frozen southern style hash brown potatoes
1 can (10¾ ounces) zesty tomato soup
½ cup water
1 teaspoon dried basil leaves
¾ teaspoon salt
¼ teaspoon pepper
¼ cup plain dry bread crumbs

Use your favorite Crisco Oil product.

1. Heat oven to 350°F. Oil 11¾×7½×2-inch baking dish lightly. Place cooling rack on countertop.

2. Heat oil in large skillet on medium-high heat. Add onion. Cook and stir until tender. Add meat. Cook until browned, stirring occasionally. Add beans. Cook and stir 5 minutes or until thawed. Add potatoes.

3. Combine tomato soup and water in small bowl. Stir until well blended. Stir into skillet. Stir in basil, salt and pepper. Spoon into baking dish. Sprinkle with bread crumbs.

4. Bake at 350°F for 30 minutes or until potatoes are tender. *Do not overbake.* Let stand 5 minutes before serving.   *Makes 4 servings*

Spaghetti Rolls

1 package (8 ounces) manicotti shells
2 pounds ground beef
1 tablespoon onion powder
1 teaspoon salt
½ teaspoon black pepper
2 cups spaghetti sauce, divided
1 cup (4 ounces) shredded pizza-flavored cheese blend or
    mozzarella cheese

1. Cook pasta according to package directions. Place in colander, then rinse under warm running water. Drain well.

2. Preheat oven to 350°F. Grease 13×9-inch baking pan.

3. Cook beef in large skillet over medium-high heat until brown, stirring to separate meat; drain drippings. Stir in onion powder, salt and pepper. Stir in 1 cup spaghetti sauce; cool and set aside.

4. Reserve ½ cup ground beef mixture. Combine remaining beef mixture with cheese in large bowl. Fill shells with remaining beef mixture using spoon.

5. Arrange shells in prepared pan. Combine remaining 1 cup spaghetti sauce with reserved beef mixture in small bowl; blend well. Pour over shells. Cover with foil.

6. Bake 20 to 30 minutes or until hot. Garnish as desired.

Makes 4 servings

Spaghetti Rolls

Chipotle Tamale Pie

¾ **pound lean ground beef or ground turkey breast**
1 **cup chopped onion**
¾ **cup diced green bell pepper**
¾ **cup diced red bell pepper**
4 **cloves garlic, minced**
2 **teaspoons ground cumin**
1 **can (15 ounces) pinto or red beans, rinsed and drained**
1 **can (8 ounces) no-salt-added stewed tomatoes, undrained**
2 **canned chipotle chilies in adobo sauce, minced (about**
    1 **tablespoon)**
1 **to 2 teaspoons adobo sauce from canned chilies (optional)**
1 **cup (4 ounces) shredded Cheddar cheese**
½ **cup chopped fresh cilantro**
1 **package (8½ ounces) corn bread mix**
⅓ **cup milk**
1 **large egg white**

1. Preheat oven to 400°F.

2. Cook beef, onion, bell peppers and garlic in large nonstick skillet over medium-high heat 8 minutes or until beef is no longer pink, stirring occasionally. Drain fat; sprinkle mixture with cumin.

3. Add beans, tomatoes, chilies and adobo sauce; bring to a boil over high heat. Reduce heat to medium; simmer, uncovered, 5 minutes. Remove from heat; stir in cheese and cilantro.

4. Spray 8-inch square baking dish with nonstick cooking spray. Spoon beef mixture evenly into prepared dish, pressing down to compact mixture. Combine corn bread mix, milk and egg white in medium bowl; mix just until dry ingredients are moistened. Spoon batter evenly over beef mixture to cover completely.

5. Bake 20 to 22 minutes or until corn bread is golden brown. Let stand 5 minutes before serving. *Makes 6 servings*

Chipotle Tamale Pie

Hearty Lasagna Rolls

1½ pounds ground beef
1 cup chopped fresh mushrooms
1 medium onion, finely chopped
1 small carrot, finely chopped
1 clove garlic, finely chopped
¼ cup dry red wine or beef broth
⅛ teaspoon cayenne pepper (optional)
2 cups shredded mozzarella cheese
1 egg, slightly beaten
5 tablespoons grated Parmesan cheese, divided
1 jar (1 pound 10 ounces) RAGÚ® Robusto! Pasta Sauce
12 ounces lasagna noodles, cooked and drained

Preheat oven to 350°F. In 12-inch skillet, brown ground beef over medium-high heat; drain. Stir in mushrooms, onion, carrot and garlic and cook over medium heat, stirring occasionally, until vegetables are tender. Stir in wine and cayenne pepper; cook over high heat 3 minutes. Remove from heat; let stand 10 minutes.

In medium bowl, thoroughly combine ground beef mixture, mozzarella cheese, egg and 2 tablespoons Parmesan cheese. In 13×9-inch baking dish, evenly pour 2 cups Ragú Robusto! Pasta Sauce. Evenly spread ⅓ cup ground beef filling over each lasagna noodle. Carefully roll up noodles. Place seam-side-down in baking dish. Evenly spread remaining sauce over lasagna rolls. Bake covered 40 minutes. Sprinkle with remaining 3 tablespoons Parmesan cheese and bake uncovered 5 minutes or until bubbling.   *Makes 6 servings*

Hearty Lasagna Rolls

Fiesta Beef Enchiladas

- **8 ounces lean ground beef**
- **½ cup sliced green onions**
- **2 teaspoons fresh minced garlic**
- **1 cup cold cooked white or brown rice**
- **1½ cups chopped tomato, divided**
- **¾ cup frozen corn, thawed**
- **1 cup (4 ounces) shredded Mexican cheese blend or Cheddar cheese, divided**
- **½ cup salsa or picante sauce**
- **12 (6- to 7-inch) corn tortillas**
- **Nonstick cooking spray**
- **1 can (10 ounces) mild or hot enchilada sauce**
- **1 cup sliced romaine lettuce leaves**

1. Preheat oven to 375°F. Cook ground beef in medium nonstick skillet over medium heat until no longer pink; drain. Add green onions and garlic; cook and stir 2 minutes.

2. Combine meat mixture, rice, 1 cup tomato, corn, ½ cup cheese and salsa; mix well. Spoon mixture down center of tortillas. Roll up; place seam side down in 13×9-inch baking dish that has been sprayed with cooking spray. Spoon enchilada sauce evenly over filled tortillas.

3. Cover with foil; bake for 20 minutes or until hot. Sprinkle with remaining ½ cup cheese; bake 5 minutes or until cheese melts. Top with lettuce and remaining ½ cup tomato.   *Makes 4 servings*

Prep Time: 15 minutes
Cook Time: 35 minutes

Fiesta Beef Enchiladas

Pizza Pie Meatloaf

2 pounds ground beef
1½ cups shredded mozzarella cheese, divided
½ cup unseasoned dry breadcrumbs
1 cup tomato sauce, divided
¼ cup grated Parmesan cheese
¼ cup *French's*® Worcestershire Sauce
1 tablespoon dried oregano leaves
1⅓ cups *French's*® French Fried Onions

1. Preheat oven to 350°F. Combine beef, *½ cup* mozzarella, bread crumbs, *½ cup* tomato sauce, Parmesan cheese, Worcestershire and oregano in large bowl; stir with fork until well blended.

2. Place meat mixture into round pizza pan with edge or pie plate and shape into 9×1-inch round. Bake 35 minutes or until no longer pink in center and internal temperature reads 160°F. Drain fat.

3. Top with remaining tomato sauce, mozzarella cheese and French Fried Onions. Bake 5 minutes or until cheese is melted and onions are golden. Cut into wedges to serve.   *Makes 6 to 8 servings*

Prep Time: 10 minutes
Cook Time: 40 minutes

Pizza Pie Meatloaf

Tacos in Pasta Shells

1 package (3 ounces) cream cheese with chives
18 jumbo pasta shells
1¼ pounds ground beef
1 teaspoon salt
1 teaspoon chili powder
2 tablespoons butter, melted
1 cup prepared taco sauce
1 cup (4 ounces) shredded Cheddar cheese
1 cup (4 ounces) shredded Monterey Jack cheese
1½ cups crushed tortilla chips
1 cup sour cream
3 green onions, chopped
Leaf lettuce, small pitted ripe olives and cherry tomatoes for garnish

1. Cut cream cheese into ½-inch cubes. Let stand at room temperature until softened. Cook pasta according to package directions. Place in colander and rinse under warm running water. Drain well. Return to saucepan.

2. Preheat oven to 350°F. Butter 13×9-inch baking pan.

3. Cook beef in large skillet over medium-high heat until brown, stirring to separate meat; drain drippings. Reduce heat to medium-low. Add cream cheese, salt and chili powder; simmer 5 minutes.

4. Toss shells with butter. Fill shells with beef mixture using spoon. Arrange shells in prepared pan. Pour taco sauce over each shell. Cover with foil.

5. Bake 15 minutes. Uncover; top with Cheddar cheese, Monterey Jack cheese and chips. Bake 15 minutes more or until bubbly. Top with sour cream and onions. Garnish, if desired.   *Makes 4 to 6 servings*

Tacos in Pasta Shells

Greek-Style Lasagna

1 pound ground beef
1 cup chopped onion
1 clove garlic, crushed OR ¼ teaspoon LAWRY'S® Garlic Powder
   with Parsley
1 teaspoon LAWRY'S® Seasoned Salt
½ teaspoon LAWRY'S® Seasoned Pepper
1 package (1.5 ounces) LAWRY'S® Original-Style Spaghetti Sauce
   Spices & Seasonings
1 can (6 ounces) tomato paste
2 cups water
¼ cup flour
½ teaspoon LAWRY'S® Seasoned Salt
1 eggplant
¾ cup salad oil
1 cup grated Parmesan cheese

In large skillet, cook ground beef until browned and crumbly; drain
fat. Add onion, garlic, 1 teaspoon Seasoned Salt, Seasoned Pepper,
Original-Style Spaghetti Sauce Spices & Seasonings, tomato paste
and water. Bring to a boil over medium-high heat, reduce heat to
low, cover and simmer 15 minutes, stirring occasionally. Meanwhile,
in small bowl, combine flour and ½ teaspoon Seasoned Salt. Peel
eggplant and slice crosswise into ¼-inch-thick slices. Place small
amount of salad oil in medium skillet and heat. Lightly coat eggplant
slices with seasoned flour. Quickly cook eggplant slices over medium-
high heat, adding oil as necessary. (Use as little oil as possible). Pour
¼ of meat sauce into a 12×8×2-inch baking dish. Cover meat sauce
with ⅓ of eggplant slices. Sprinkle ¼ of Parmesan cheese over
eggplant. Repeat layers 2 more times, ending with meat sauce and
Parmesan cheese. Bake, uncovered, in 350 F. oven 30 minutes.

Makes 6 to 8 servings

Serving Suggestion: Serve with tossed green salad and fruit dessert.

Mexican Stuffed Shells

  1 pound ground beef
  1 jar (12 ounces) mild or medium picante sauce
  ½ cup water
  1 can (8 ounces) tomato sauce
  1 can (4 ounces) chopped green chilies, drained
  1 cup (4 ounces) shredded Monterey Jack cheese, divided
1⅓ cups *French's®* French Fried Onions
 12 pasta stuffing shells, cooked in unsalted water and drained

Preheat oven to 350°F. In large skillet, brown ground beef; drain. In small bowl, combine picante sauce, water and tomato sauce. Stir ½ cup sauce mixture into beef along with chilies, ½ cup cheese and ⅔ *cup* French Fried Onions; mix well. Spread half the remaining sauce mixture in bottom of 10-inch round baking dish. Stuff cooked shells with beef mixture. Arrange shells in baking dish; top with remaining sauce. Bake, covered, at 350°F for 30 minutes or until heated through. Top with remaining ⅔ *cup* onions and cheese; bake, uncovered, 5 minutes or until cheese is melted.   *Makes 6 servings*

Microwave Directions: Crumble ground beef into medium microwave-safe bowl. Cook, covered, on HIGH (100%) 4 to 6 minutes or until beef is cooked. Stir beef halfway through cooking time. Drain well. Prepare sauce mixture as above; spread ½ cup in 12×8-inch microwave-safe dish. Prepare beef mixture as above. Stuff cooked shells with beef mixture. Arrange shells in dish; top with remaining sauce. Cook, covered, 10 to 12 minutes or until heated through. Rotate dish halfway through cooking time. Top with remaining onions and cheese; cook, uncovered, 1 minute or until cheese is melted. Let stand 5 minutes.

Tamale Pie

1 tablespoon olive or vegetable oil
1 small onion, chopped
1 pound ground beef
1 envelope LIPTON® RECIPE SECRETS® Onion Soup Mix*
1 can (14½ ounces) stewed tomatoes, undrained
½ cup water
1 can (15 to 19 ounces) red kidney beans, rinsed and drained
1 package (8½ ounces) corn muffin mix

*Also terrific with LIPTON® RECIPE SECRETS® Fiesta Herb with Red Pepper, Onion-Mushroom, Beefy Onion or Beefy Mushroom Soup Mix.

• Preheat oven to 400°F.

• In 12-inch skillet, heat oil over medium heat and cook onion, stirring occasionally, 3 minutes or until tender. Stir in ground beef and cook until browned.

• Stir in onion soup mix blended with tomatoes and water. Bring to a boil over high heat, stirring with spoon to crush tomatoes. Reduce heat to low and stir in beans. Simmer uncovered, stirring occasionally, 10 minutes. Turn into 2-quart casserole.

• Prepare corn muffin mix according to package directions. Spoon evenly over casserole.

• Bake uncovered 15 minutes or until corn topping is golden and filling is hot.   *Makes about 6 servings*

Tamale Pie

Cheddar Burger Mashed Potato Bake

2 pounds ground beef
1 medium onion, chopped
1 jar (16 ounces) RAGÚ® Cheese Creations!® Double Cheddar Sauce
2 teaspoons dry mustard
4 cups prepared mashed potatoes

Preheat oven to 425°F. In 12-inch skillet, brown ground beef over medium-high heat; drain. Add onion and cook, stirring occasionally, 2 minutes. Stir in Ragú Cheese Creations! Sauce, mustard and, if desired, salt and ground black pepper to taste. Simmer uncovered, stirring occasionally, 3 minutes or until heated through.

Turn into 2-quart casserole; evenly top with mashed potatoes. Bake uncovered 25 minutes or until potatoes are lightly golden.

Makes 8 servings

Recipe Tip: When making mashed potatoes, use Idaho or all-purpose potatoes for marvelous flavor and texture. Heat the milk before adding it—this minimizes any starchiness.

Cheddar Burger Mashed Potato Bake

Chili Spaghetti Casserole

8 ounces uncooked spaghetti
1 pound lean ground beef
1 medium onion, chopped
¼ teaspoon salt
⅛ teaspoon black pepper
1 can (15 ounces) vegetarian chili with beans
1 can (14½ ounces) Italian-style stewed tomatoes, undrained
1½ cups (6 ounces) shredded sharp Cheddar cheese, divided
½ cup reduced-fat sour cream
1½ teaspoons chili powder
¼ teaspoon garlic powder

Preheat oven to 350°F. Spray 13×9-inch baking dish with nonstick cooking spray.

Cook pasta according to package directions until al dente. Drain and place in prepared dish.

Meanwhile, place beef and onion in large skillet; season with salt and pepper. Brown beef over medium-high heat until beef is no longer pink, stirring to separate meat. Drain fat. Stir in chili, tomatoes with juice, 1 cup cheese, sour cream, chili powder and garlic powder.

Add chili mixture to pasta; stir until pasta is well coated. Sprinkle with remaining ½ cup cheese.

Cover tightly with foil and bake 30 minutes or until hot and bubbly. Let stand 5 minutes before serving.   *Makes 8 servings*

Chili Spaghetti Casserole

Patchwork Casserole

2 pounds ground beef
2 cups chopped green bell pepper
1 cup chopped onion
2 pounds frozen Southern-style hash-brown potatoes, thawed
2 cans (8 ounces each) tomato sauce
1 cup water
1 can (6 ounces) tomato paste
1 teaspoon salt
½ teaspoon dried basil, crumbled
¼ teaspoon black pepper
1 pound pasteurized process American cheese, thinly sliced

Preheat oven to 350°F.

Brown beef in large skillet over medium heat about 10 minutes; drain off fat.

Add bell pepper and onion; cook and stir until tender, about 4 minutes. Stir in potatoes, tomato sauce, water, tomato paste, salt, basil and black pepper.

Spoon half of mixture into 13×9×2-inch baking pan or 3-quart baking dish; top with half of cheese. Spoon remaining meat mixture evenly on top of cheese. Cover pan with aluminum foil. Bake 45 minutes.

Cut remaining cheese into decorative shapes; place on top of casserole. Let stand loosely covered until cheese melts, about 5 minutes.   *Makes 8 to 10 servings*

Patchwork Casserole

Saucy Stuffed Peppers

6 medium green bell peppers
1¼ cups water
2 cups low-sodium tomato juice, divided
1 can (6 ounces) tomato paste
1 teaspoon dried oregano leaves, crushed, divided
½ teaspoon dried basil leaves, crushed
½ teaspoon garlic powder, divided
1 pound lean ground beef
1½ cups QUAKER® Oats (quick or old fashioned, uncooked)
1 medium tomato, chopped
¼ cup chopped carrot
¼ cup chopped onion

Heat oven to 350°F. Cut peppers lengthwise in half. Remove membranes and seeds; set peppers aside. In large saucepan, combine water, 1 cup tomato juice, tomato paste, ½ teaspoon oregano, basil and ¼ teaspoon garlic powder. Simmer 10 to 15 minutes.

Combine beef, oats, remaining 1 cup tomato juice, ½ teaspoon oregano and ¼ teaspoon garlic powder with tomato, carrot and onion; mix well. Fill each pepper half with about ⅓ cup meat mixture. Place in 13×9-inch glass baking dish; pour sauce evenly over peppers. Bake 45 to 50 minutes.   *Makes 12 servings*

Spinach-Potato Bake

1 pound ground beef
½ cup sliced fresh mushrooms
1 small onion, chopped
2 cloves garlic, minced
1 package (10 ounces) frozen chopped spinach, thawed, well
    drained
½ teaspoon ground nutmeg
1 pound russet potatoes, peeled, cooked and mashed
¼ cup light sour cream
¼ cup fat-free (skim) milk
   Salt and black pepper
½ cup (2 ounces) shredded Cheddar cheese

Preheat oven to 400°F. Spray deep 9-inch casserole dish with nonstick cooking spray.

Brown ground beef in large skillet. Drain. Add mushrooms, onion and garlic; cook until tender. Stir in spinach and nutmeg; cover. Heat thoroughly, stirring occasionally.

Combine potatoes, sour cream and milk. Add to ground beef mixture; season with salt and pepper to taste. Spoon into prepared casserole dish; sprinkle with cheese.

Bake 15 to 20 minutes or until slightly puffed and cheese is melted.
Makes 6 servings

Silly Spaghetti Casserole

 8 ounces dried spaghetti
¼ cup cholesterol-free egg substitute
¼ cup finely shredded Parmesan cheese
½ (10-ounce) package frozen cut spinach, thawed
¾ pound lean ground beef or turkey
⅓ cup chopped onion
 2 cups prepared spaghetti sauce
¾ cup shredded part-skim mozzarella cheese (3 ounces)
 1 green or yellow bell pepper

1. Preheat oven to 350°F. Spray 8-inch square baking dish with nonstick cooking spray.

2. Cook spaghetti according to package directions; drain. Toss with egg substitute and Parmesan cheese. Place in bottom of prepared baking dish.

3. Drain spinach in colander, pressing out excess liquid. Spray large nonstick skillet with cooking spray. Cook beef and onion in skillet over medium-high heat until meat is lightly browned, stirring to break up meat. Drain off fat. Stir in spinach and spaghetti sauce. Spoon on top of spaghetti mixture.

4. Sprinkle with mozzarella cheese. Use small cookie cutter to cut decorative shapes from bell pepper. Place on top of cheese in baking dish. Cover dish with foil. Bake 40 to 45 minutes or until bubbling. Let stand 10 minutes. Cut into squares.   *Makes 6 servings*

Silly Spaghetti Casserole

California Tamale Pie

- 1 pound ground beef
- 1 cup yellow corn meal
- 2 cups milk
- 2 eggs, beaten
- 1 package (1.48 ounces) LAWRY'S® Spices & Seasonings for Chili
- 2 teaspoons LAWRY'S® Seasoned Salt
- 1 can (17 ounces) whole kernel corn, drained
- 1 can (14½ ounces) whole tomatoes, cut up
- 1 can (2¼ ounces) sliced ripe olives, drained
- 1 cup (4 ounces) shredded cheddar cheese

In medium skillet, cook ground beef until browned and crumbly; drain fat. In 2½-quart casserole dish, combine corn meal, milk and eggs; mix well. Add ground beef and remaining ingredients except cheese; stir to mix. Bake, uncovered, in 350°F oven 1 hour and 15 minutes. Add cheese and continue baking until cheese melts. Let stand 10 minutes before serving.

MICROWAVE OVEN METHOD
In 2½-quart glass casserole, microwave ground beef on HIGH 5 to 6 minutes; drain fat and crumble beef. Mix in corn meal, milk and eggs; blend well. Add remaining ingredients except cheese. Cover with plastic wrap, venting one corner. Microwave on HIGH 15 minutes, stirring after 8 minutes. Sprinkle cheese over top and microwave on HIGH 2 minutes. Let stand 10 minutes before serving.

Makes 6 to 8 servings

Serving Suggestion: Serve with mixed green salad flavored with kiwi and green onion.

Hint: Substitute 1 package (1.25 ounces) LAWRY'S® Taco Spices & Seasonings for Spices & Seasonings for Chili Seasoning Mix, if desired.

California Tamale Pie

Simple
SKILLET DISHES

Italian Beef Burrito

1½ **pounds ground beef**
  2 **medium onions, finely chopped**
  2 **medium red and/or green bell peppers, chopped**
  1 **jar (26 to 28 ounces) RAGÚ® Robusto!™ Pasta Sauce**
½ **teaspoon dried oregano leaves, crushed**
  8 **(10-inch) flour tortillas, warmed**
  2 **cups shredded mozzarella cheese (about 8 ounces)**

1. In 12-inch skillet, brown ground beef over medium-high heat.

2. Stir in onions and red bell peppers and cook, stirring occasionally, 5 minutes or until tender; drain. Stir in Ragú Pasta Sauce and oregano; heat through.

3. To serve, top each tortilla with ¼ cup cheese and 1 cup ground beef mixture; roll up and serve.

Makes 8 servings

Prep Time: 15 minutes
Cook Time: 15 minutes

Italian Beef Burrito

Velveeta® Cheeseburger Mac

1 pound ground beef
2¾ cups water
⅓ cup catsup
1 to 2 teaspoons onion powder
2 cups (8 ounces) elbow macaroni, uncooked
¾ pound (12 ounces) VELVEETA® Pasteurized Prepared Cheese
    Product, cut up

1. Brown meat in large skillet; drain.

2. Stir in water, catsup and onion powder. Bring to boil. Stir in macaroni. Reduce heat to medium-low; cover. Simmer 8 to 10 minutes or until macaroni is tender.

3. Add VELVEETA; stir until melted.   *Makes 4 to 6 servings*

Safe Food Handling: Store ground beef in the coldest part of the refrigerator for up to 2 days. Make sure raw juices do not touch other foods. Ground meat can be wrapped airtight and frozen for up to 3 months.

Prep Time: 10 minutes
Cook Time: 15 minutes

Velveeta® Cheeseburger Mac

Malaysian Curried Beef

2 tablespoons vegetable oil
2 large yellow onions, chopped
1 piece fresh ginger (about 1 inch square), minced
2 cloves garlic, minced
2 tablespoons curry powder
1 teaspoon salt
2 large baking potatoes (1 pound), peeled and cut into chunks
1 cup beef broth
1 pound ground beef chuck
2 ripe tomatoes (12 ounces), peeled and cut into chunks
　Hot cooked rice
　Purple kale and watercress sprigs for garnish

1. Heat wok over medium-high heat 1 minute or until hot. Drizzle oil into wok and heat 30 seconds. Add onions and stir-fry 2 minutes. Add ginger, garlic, curry and salt to wok. Cook and stir about 1 minute or until fragrant. Add potatoes; cook and stir 2 to 3 minutes.

2. Add beef broth to potato mixture. Cover and bring to a boil. Reduce heat to low; simmer about 20 minutes or until potatoes are fork-tender.

3. Stir ground beef into potato mixture. Cook and stir about 5 minutes or until beef is browned and no pink remains; spoon off fat if necessary.

4. Add tomato chunks and stir gently until thoroughly heated. Spoon beef mixture into serving dish. Top center with rice. Garnish, if desired. *Makes 4 servings*

Malaysian Curried Beef

Ragú® Chili Mac

1 tablespoon olive or vegetable oil
1 medium green bell pepper, chopped
1 pound ground beef
1 jar (26 to 28 ounces) RAGÚ® Old World Style® Pasta Sauce
2 tablespoons chili powder
8 ounces elbow macaroni, cooked and drained

1. In 12-inch nonstick skillet, heat oil over medium-high heat and cook green bell pepper, stirring occasionally, 3 minutes. Add ground beef and brown, stirring occasionally; drain.

2. Stir in Ragú Pasta Sauce and chili powder. Bring to a boil over high heat. Reduce heat to low and simmer covered 10 minutes.

3. Stir in macaroni and heat through. Serve, if desired, with sour cream and shredded Cheddar cheese.   *Makes 4 servings*

Prep Time: 10 minutes
Cook Time: 25 minutes

Tip. Store ground beef in the coldest part of the refrigerator for up to 2 days, or wrap it airtight and freeze for up to 3 months.

Ragú® Chili Mac

Mexican Skillet Rice

¾ **pound lean ground beef or lean ground pork**
1 **medium onion, chopped**
1½ **tablespoons chili powder**
1 **teaspoon ground cumin**
½ **teaspoon salt**
3 **cups cooked brown rice**
1 **can (16 ounces) pinto beans, drained**
2 **cans (4 ounces each) diced green chilies**
1 **medium tomato, seeded and chopped (optional)**

Cook meat in large skillet over medium-high heat until brown, stirring to crumble; drain. Return meat to skillet. Add onion, chili powder, cumin and salt; cook until onion is soft but not brown. Stir in rice, beans, and chilies; heat through. Top with tomato, if desired.

Makes 6 servings

Microwave Directions: Combine meat and onion in 2- to 3-quart microwavable baking dish, stirring well. Cover with waxed paper and cook on HIGH 4 to 5 minutes, stirring after 2 minutes, or until meat is no longer pink. Drain. Add chili powder, cumin, salt, rice, beans and chilies. Cook on HIGH 4 to 5 minutes, stirring after 2 minutes, or until thoroughly heated. Top with tomato, if desired.

Mexican Skillet Rice

Onion Sloppy Joes

1½ pounds ground beef
1 envelope LIPTON® RECIPE SECRETS® Onion Soup Mix
1 cup water
1 cup ketchup
2 tablespoons firmly packed brown sugar

In 10-inch skillet, brown ground beef over medium-high heat; drain.

Stir in remaining ingredients. Bring to a boil over high heat.

Reduce heat to low and simmer uncovered, stirring occasionally, 8 minutes or until mixture thickens. Serve, if desired, on hoagie rolls or hamburger buns.   *Makes about 6 servings*

Menu Suggestion: Serve with a lettuce and tomato salad, tortilla chips and ice cream with a choice of toppings.

Velveeta® 15 Minute Cheesy Chili 'n Rice Skillet

1 pound ground beef
1 can (15 ounces) chili with beans
1 can (14½ ounces) diced tomatoes, undrained
1 cup water
2 cups MINUTE® White Rice, uncooked
½ pound (8 ounces) VELVEETA® Pasteurized Prepared Cheese
        Product, cut up

1. Brown meat in large skillet on medium-high heat; drain.

2. Add chili, tomatoes and water to skillet; stir. Bring to boil.

3. Stir in rice and VELVEETA; cover. Remove from heat. Let stand 5 minutes. Stir until VELVEETA is melted.   *Makes 4 servings*

Onion Sloppy Joe

Simple Skillet Dishes

Broccoli and Beef Pasta

1 pound lean ground beef
2 cloves garlic, minced
1 can (about 14 ounces) beef broth
1 medium onion, thinly sliced
1 cup uncooked rotini pasta
½ teaspoon dried basil leaves
½ teaspoon dried oregano leaves
½ teaspoon dried thyme leaves
1 can (15 ounces) Italian-style tomatoes, undrained
2 cups broccoli florets *or* 1 package (10 ounces) frozen broccoli, thawed
3 ounces shredded Cheddar cheese or grated Parmesan cheese

1. Combine meat and garlic in large nonstick skillet; cook over high heat until meat is no longer pink, breaking meat apart with wooden spoon. Pour off drippings. Place meat in large bowl; set aside.

2. Add broth, onion, pasta, basil, oregano and thyme to skillet. Bring to a boil. Reduce heat to medium-high and boil 10 minutes (if using frozen broccoli, boil 15 minutes); add tomatoes with juice. Increase heat to high and bring to a boil; stir in broccoli. Cook, uncovered, 6 to 8 minutes, stirring occasionally, until broccoli is crisp-tender and pasta is tender. Return meat to skillet and stir 3 to 4 minutes or until heated through.

3. With slotted spoon, transfer to serving platter. Sprinkle with cheese. Cover with lid or tent with foil several minutes, until cheese melts. Meanwhile, bring liquid left in skillet to a boil over high heat. Boil until thick and reduced to 3 to 4 tablespoons. Spoon over pasta.

Makes 4 servings

Serving Suggestion: Serve with garlic bread.

Prep and Cook Time: 30 minutes

Broccoli and Beef Pasta

Simple Skillet Dishes

Skillet Spaghetti and Sausage

¼ **pound mild or hot Italian sausage links, sliced**
½ **pound ground beef**
¼ **teaspoon dried oregano, crushed**
 4 **ounces spaghetti, broken in half**
 1 **can (14½ ounces) DEL MONTE® Diced Tomatoes with Basil,**
    Garlic & Oregano
 1 **can (8 ounces) DEL MONTE® Tomato Sauce**
1½ **cups sliced fresh mushrooms**
 2 **stalks celery, sliced**

1. Brown sausage in large skillet over medium-high heat. Add beef and oregano; season to taste with salt and pepper, if desired.

2. Cook, stirring occasionally, until beef is browned; drain.

3. Add pasta, 1 cup water, undrained tomatoes, tomato sauce, mushrooms and celery. Bring to boil, stirring occasionally.

4. Reduce heat; cover and simmer 12 to 14 minutes or until spaghetti is tender. Garnish with grated Parmesan cheese and chopped parsley, if desired. Serve immediately. *Makes 4 to 6 servings*

Prep Time: 5 minutes
Cook Time: 30 minutes

Simple Skillet Dishes

Pasta Beef & Zucchini Dinner

1 pound extra-lean ground beef
1 medium onion, chopped
1 clove garlic, crushed
½ teaspoon salt
2 (14-ounce) cans ready-to-serve beef broth
1 teaspoon Italian seasoning
¼ teaspoon crushed red pepper
2 cups uncooked mini lasagna or rotini pasta
2 cups sliced zucchini (cut ⅜ inch thick)
1 tablespoon cornstarch
¼ cup water
3 plum tomatoes, each cut into 4 wedges
2 tablespoons grated Parmesan cheese

In large nonstick skillet, cook ground beef with onion, garlic and salt over medium heat 8 to 10 minutes or until beef is browned, stirring occasionally to break up beef into 1-inch crumbles. Remove beef mixture with slotted spoon; pour off drippings. Set aside.

Add broth, Italian seasoning and red pepper to same skillet. Bring to a boil; add pasta. Reduce heat to medium; simmer, uncovered, for 6 minutes, stirring occasionally. Add zucchini; continue cooking for an additional 6 to 8 minutes or until pasta is tender yet firm. Push pasta and zucchini to side of skillet. Mix cornstarch with water and add to broth in skillet; bring to a boil. Return beef mixture to skillet. Add tomatoes; heat through, stirring occasionally. Spoon into serving dish; sprinkle with Parmesan cheese.   *Makes 5 servings*

*Favorite recipe from **North Dakota Wheat Commission***

Greek Beef & Rice

1 bag SUCCESS® Rice
1 pound lean ground beef
2 medium zucchini, sliced
½ cup chopped onion
1 medium clove garlic, minced
1 can (14½ ounces) tomato sauce
¾ teaspoon dried basil leaves, crushed
¾ teaspoon salt
¼ teaspoon pepper

Prepare rice according to package directions.

Brown beef in large skillet, stirring occasionally to separate beef. Pour off all but 2 tablespoons drippings. Add zucchini, onion and garlic to skillet; cook and stir until crisp-tender. Add all remaining ingredients *except* rice; cover. Simmer 10 minutes, stirring occasionally. Add rice; heat thoroughly, stirring occasionally. Garnish, if desired.

Makes 6 servings

Be sure to choose firm, bright-colored zucchini that are free of spots and bruises. Store zucchini in a plastic bag in the refrigerator for up to five days.

Greek Beef & Rice

Curry Beef

12 ounces wide egg noodles *or* **1⅓ cups long-grain white rice**
1 tablespoon olive oil
1 medium onion, thinly sliced
1 tablespoon curry powder
1 teaspoon ground cumin
2 cloves garlic, minced
1 pound lean ground beef
1 cup (8 ounces) sour cream
½ cup 2% milk
½ cup raisins, divided
1 teaspoon sugar
¼ cup chopped walnuts, almonds or pecans

1. Cook noodles or rice according to package directions. Meanwhile, heat oil in large skillet over medium-high heat until hot. Add onion; cook and stir 3 to 4 minutes. Add curry powder, cumin and garlic; cook 2 to 3 minutes longer or until onion is tender. Add meat; cook 6 to 8 minutes or until meat is no longer pink, breaking meat apart with wooden spoon.

2. Stir in sour cream, milk, ¼ cup raisins and sugar. Reduce heat to medium; cook, stirring constantly, until heated through. Spoon over drained noodles or rice. Sprinkle with remaining ¼ cup raisins and nuts. *Makes 4 servings*

Serving Suggestion: Serve with sliced cucumber sprinkled with sugar and vinegar or plain yogurt topped with brown sugar, chopped bananas and green onions.

Prep and Cook Time: 30 minutes

Curry Beef

Chuckwagon BBQ Rice Round-Up

1 pound lean ground beef
1 (6.8-ounce) package RICE-A-RONI® Beef Flavor
2 tablespoons margarine or butter
2 cups frozen corn
½ cup prepared barbecue sauce
½ cup (2 ounces) shredded Cheddar cheese

1. In large skillet over medium-high heat, brown ground beef until well cooked. Remove from skillet; drain. Set aside.

2. In same skillet over medium heat, sauté rice-vermicelli mix with margarine until vermicelli is golden brown.

3. Slowly stir in 2½ cups water, corn and Special Seasonings; bring to a boil. Reduce heat to low. Cover; simmer 15 to 20 minutes or until rice is tender.

4. Stir in barbecue sauce and ground beef. Sprinkle with cheese. Cover; let stand 3 to 5 minutes or until cheese is melted.

Makes 4 servings

Tip: Salsa can be substituted for barbecue sauce.

Prep Time: 5 minutes
Cook Time: 25 minutes

Chuckwagon BBQ Rice Round-Up

Quick Greek Pitas

1 pound ground beef
1 package (10 ounces) frozen chopped spinach, thawed and
   well drained
4 green onions, chopped
1 can (2¼ ounces) sliced black olives, drained
1 teaspoon dried oregano, divided
¼ teaspoon pepper
1 large tomato, diced
1 cup plain nonfat yogurt
½ cup mayonnaise
6 (6-inch) pita breads, warmed
   Lettuce leaves
1 cup (4 ounces) crumbled feta cheese

Cook and stir ground beef in large skillet over medium-high heat
until crumbly and no longer pink. Drain off drippings. Add spinach,
green onions, olives, ½ teaspoon oregano and pepper; cook and stir
2 minutes. Stir in tomato.

Combine yogurt, mayonnaise and remaining ½ teaspoon oregano
in small bowl. Split open pita breads; line each with lettuce leaf. Stir
cheese into beef mixture and divide among pita pockets. Serve with
yogurt sauce.   *Makes 6 servings*

Quick Greek Pita

Simple Skillet Dishes

Cheeseburger Macaroni

1 cup mostaccioli or elbow macaroni, uncooked
1 pound ground beef
1 medium onion, chopped
1 can (14½ ounces) DEL MONTE® Diced Tomatoes with Basil, Garlic
   & Oregano
¼ cup DEL MONTE® Tomato Ketchup
1 cup (4 ounces) shredded Cheddar cheese

1. Cook pasta according to package directions; drain.

2. Brown meat with onion in large skillet; drain. Season with salt and pepper, if desired. Stir in undrained tomatoes, ketchup and pasta; heat through.

3. Top with cheese. Garnish, if desired.   *Makes 4 servings*

Prep Time: 8 minutes
Cook Time: 15 minutes

Tip If you'll be cooking this dish often for your kids, cook twice the amount of pasta called for and reserve it for another meal. Drain the extra portion well and toss it with a teaspoon of oil. Cover and refrigerate for up to three days.

Cheeseburger Macaroni

Taco Pot Pie

1 pound ground beef
1 package (1.25 ounces) taco seasoning mix
¼ cup water
1 can (8 ounces) kidney beans, rinsed and drained
1 cup chopped tomato
¾ cup frozen corn, thawed
¾ cup frozen peas, thawed
1½ cups (6 ounces) shredded Cheddar cheese
1 can (11.5 ounces) refrigerated corn breadstick dough

1. Preheat oven to 400°F. Brown meat in medium ovenproof skillet over medium-high heat, stirring to separate; drain drippings. Add seasoning mix and water to skillet. Cook over medium-low heat 3 minutes or until most of liquid is absorbed, stirring occasionally.

2. Stir in beans, tomato, corn and peas. Cook 3 minutes or until mixture is hot. Remove from heat; stir in cheese.

3. Unwrap corn bread dough; separate into 16 strips. Twist strips, cutting to fit skillet. Arrange attractively over meat mixture. Press ends of dough lightly to edge of skillet to secure. Bake 15 minutes or until corn bread is golden brown and meat mixture is bubbly.

Makes 4 to 6 servings

Prep and Cook Time: 30 minutes

Taco Pot Pie

Beef with Snow Peas & Baby Corn

¾ **pound extra-lean ground beef**
1 **clove garlic, minced**
1 **teaspoon vegetable oil**
6 **ounces snow peas, halved lengthwise**
1 **red bell pepper, cut into strips**
1 **can (15 ounces) baby corn, drained and rinsed**
1 **tablespoon soy sauce**
1 **teaspoon sesame oil**
  Salt and black pepper
2 **cups cooked rice**

Brown ground beef in wok or large skillet. Drain. Add garlic; cook until tender. Set aside. Wipe out wok with paper towel.

Heat vegetable oil in wok over medium-high heat. Add snow peas and red bell pepper; stir-fry 2 to 3 minutes or until vegetables are crisp-tender. Stir in ground beef mixture, baby corn, soy sauce and sesame oil; cook until heated through. Season with salt and black pepper to taste. Serve over rice.   *Makes 4 servings*

Tip

Baby corn is a popular ingredient in Asian cooking. It is available in cans or jars, and it is found in the canned vegetable or ethnic section of most supermarkets.

Beef with Snow Peas & Baby Corn

Tijuana Tacos

- 1 teaspoon vegetable oil
- ½ cup chopped green bell pepper
- ½ cup chopped green onions
- 1 jalapeño pepper,* minced
- 1 pound lean ground beef
- 1 cup salsa
- ½ teaspoon ground cumin
- ½ teaspoon chili powder
- 8 taco shells
- 2 cups shredded lettuce
- 2 cups chopped tomato
- 1½ cups (6 ounces) shredded Cheddar cheese

Jalapeño peppers can sting and irritate the skin; wear rubber gloves when handling peppers and do not touch eyes.

Heat oil in large nonstick skillet over medium-high heat until hot. Add bell pepper, onions and jalapeño pepper; cook and stir 5 minutes or until vegetables are tender.

Add beef to vegetable mixture. Cook until no longer pink; pour off excess fat. Add salsa, cumin and chili powder to meat mixture; stir to combine.

Spoon beef mixture into taco shells. Top with lettuce, tomato and Cheddar cheese. Garnish as desired.   *Makes 8 servings*

Tijuana Tacos

Tex-Mex Beef & Black Bean Skillet

1 pound lean ground beef or ground turkey
1 medium onion, chopped
2 cloves garlic, minced
1 tablespoon Mexican seasoning*
1 (6.8-ounce) package RICE-A-RONI® Spanish Rice
2 tablespoons margarine or butter
1 (16-ounce) jar salsa *or* 1 (14½-ounce) can diced tomatoes and
    green chiles, undrained
1 (16-ounce) can black beans, rinsed and drained
1 cup shredded Monterey Jack cheese or jalapeño pepper

*1 teaspoon chili powder, 1 teaspoon ground cumin, 1 teaspoon garlic salt and
¼ teaspoon cayenne pepper may be substituted.*

1. In large skillet over medium-high heat, cook ground beef, onion and garlic until meat is no longer pink, stirring frequently. Drain; transfer to bowl. Toss with Mexican seasoning; set aside.

2. In same skillet over medium heat, sauté rice-vermicelli mix with margarine until vermicelli is golden brown.

3. Slowly stir in 2 cups water, salsa and Special Seasonings; bring to a boil. Cover; reduce heat to low. Simmer 10 minutes.

4. Stir in beef mixture and beans. Cover; simmer 8 to 10 minutes or until rice is tender. Top with cheese.   *Makes 6 servings*

Prep Time: 10 minutes
Cook Time: 25 minutes

Szechwan Beef

1 pound ground beef
1 tablespoon vegetable oil
1 cup sliced carrots
1 cup frozen peas
⅓ cup water
3 tablespoons soy sauce
2 tablespoons cornstarch
¼ teaspoon ground ginger
1 jar (7 ounces) baby corn
1 medium onion, thinly sliced
   Sliced mushrooms and olives as desired
¼ cup shredded Cheddar cheese
1⅓ cups uncooked instant rice

1. In wok or large skillet, brown ground beef; remove from wok and set aside. Drain fat.

2. Add oil to wok or skillet and return to medium heat. Add carrots and peas and stir-fry about 3 minutes.

3. In small cup blend water, soy sauce, cornstarch and ginger. Add to vegetables in wok.

4. Return ground beef to wok along with baby corn, onion, mushrooms, olives and cheese. Cook over medium heat until all ingredients are heated through.

5. Prepare instant rice according to package directions. Serve beef and vegetables over rice.   *Makes 4 to 5 servings*

Favorite recipe from **North Dakota Beef Commission**

Simple Skillet Dishes

Soups,
STEWS & CHILIS

Rapid Ragú® Chili

1½ pounds lean ground beef
  1 medium onion, chopped
  2 tablespoons chili powder
  1 can (19 ounces) red kidney beans, rinsed and drained
  1 jar (26 to 28 ounces) RAGÚ® Old World Style® Pasta Sauce
  1 cup shredded Cheddar cheese (about 4 ounces)

1. In 12-inch skillet, brown ground beef with onion and chili powder over medium-high heat, stirring occasionally. Stir in beans and Ragú Pasta Sauce.

2. Bring to a boil over high heat. Reduce heat to low and simmer covered, stirring occasionally, 20 minutes. Top with cheese. Serve, if desired, over hot cooked rice.

Makes 6 servings

Prep Time: 10 minutes
Cook Time: 25 minutes

Rapid Ragú® Chili

All-in-One Burger Stew

1 pound lean ground beef
2 cups frozen Italian vegetables
1 can (14½ ounces) chopped tomatoes with basil and garlic,
   undrained
1 can (about 14 ounces) beef broth
2½ cups uncooked medium egg noodles
   Salt and black pepper

1. Cook meat in Dutch oven or large skillet over medium-high heat until no longer pink, stirring to separate meat. Drain drippings.

2. Add vegetables, tomatoes with juice and broth; bring to a boil over high heat.

3. Add noodles; reduce heat to medium. Cover and cook 12 to 15 minutes or until noodles have absorbed liquid and vegetables are tender. Add salt and pepper to taste. *Makes 6 servings*

Note: For a special touch, sprinkle with chopped parsley before serving.

Tip: To complete this meal, serve with breadsticks or a loaf of Italian bread and a mixed green and tomato salad.

Prep and Cook Time: 25 minutes

All-in-One Burger Stew

Chile con Carne

2 tablespoons vegetable oil

2 pounds ground beef

2 cups (2 small) chopped onions

4 cloves garlic, finely chopped

3½ cups (two 15-ounce cans) kidney, pinto or black beans, drained

3½ cups (29-ounce can) crushed tomatoes

1¾ cups (16-ounce jar) ORTEGA® Salsa Prima-Thick & Chunky Mild

½ cup dry white wine

½ cup (4-ounce can) ORTEGA® Diced Green Chiles

3 tablespoons chili powder

1 to 2 tablespoons ORTEGA® Diced Jalapeños

1 tablespoon ground cumin

1 tablespoon dried oregano, crushed

2 teaspoons salt

HEAT vegetable oil in large saucepan over medium-high heat. Add beef, onions and garlic; cook for 4 to 5 minutes or until beef is no longer pink; drain.

STIR in beans, crushed tomatoes, salsa, wine, chiles, chili powder, jalapeños, cumin, oregano and salt. Bring to a boil. Reduce heat to low; cover. Cook, stirring frequently, for 1 hour.

Makes 10 to 12 servings

Chile con Carne

Ground Beef, Spinach and Barley Soup

12 ounces lean ground beef
4 cups water
1 can (14½ ounces) no-salt-added stewed tomatoes, undrained
1½ cups thinly sliced carrots
1 cup chopped onion
½ cup quick-cooking barley
1½ teaspoons beef bouillon granules
1½ teaspoons dried thyme leaves, crushed
1 teaspoon dried oregano leaves, crushed
½ teaspoon garlic powder
¼ teaspoon black pepper
⅛ teaspoon salt
3 cups torn stemmed and washed spinach leaves

Cook beef in large saucepan over medium heat until no longer pink, stirring to separate. Drain drippings. Stir in water, stewed tomatoes with juice, carrots, onion, barley, bouillon granules, thyme, oregano, garlic powder, pepper and salt.

Bring to a boil over high heat. Reduce heat to medium-low. Cover and simmer 12 to 15 minutes or until barley and vegetables are tender, stirring occasionally. Stir in spinach; cook until spinach starts to wilt.

Makes 4 servings

Ground Beef, Spinach and Barley Soup

Hamburger Soup

1 pound lean ground beef
1 envelope (1 ounce) dried onion soup mix
1 envelope (1 ounce) Italian seasoning mix
¼ teaspoon seasoned salt
¼ teaspoon black pepper
3 cups boiling water
1 can (8 ounces) diced tomatoes, undrained
1 can (8 ounces) tomato sauce
1 tablespoon soy sauce
1 cup sliced celery
1 cup thinly sliced carrots
2 cups cooked macaroni
¼ cup grated Parmesan cheese
2 tablespoons chopped fresh parsley

SLOW COOKER DIRECTIONS

1. Brown beef in medium skillet over medium-high heat; drain. Add beef to slow cooker. Add soup mix, Italian seasoning, seasoned salt and pepper. Stir in water, tomatoes with juice, tomato sauce and soy sauce. Add celery and carrots. Cover and cook on LOW 6 to 8 hours.

2. Increase heat to HIGH; stir in cooked macaroni and Parmesan cheese. Cover and cook 10 to 15 minutes. Sprinkle with parsley just before serving.   *Makes 6 to 8 servings*

Hamburger Soup

Albóndigas Soup

1 pound ground beef
¼ cup long-grain rice
1 egg
1 tablespoon chopped fresh cilantro
1 teaspoon LAWRY'S® Seasoned Salt
¼ cup ice water
2 cans (14½ ounces each) chicken broth
1 can (14½ ounces) whole peeled tomatoes, undrained and cut up
1 stalk celery, diced
1 large carrot, diced
1 medium potato, diced
¼ cup chopped onion
¼ teaspoon LAWRY'S® Garlic Powder with Parsley

In medium bowl, combine ground beef, rice, egg, cilantro, Seasoned Salt and ice water; mix well and form into small meatballs. In large saucepan, combine broth, vegetables and Garlic Powder with Parsley. Bring to a boil over medium-high heat; add meatballs. Reduce heat to low; cover and cook 30 to 40 minutes, stirring occasionally.

Makes 6 to 8 servings

Serving Suggestion: Serve with lemon wedges and warm tortillas.

Hint: For a lower salt version, use homemade chicken broth or low-sodium chicken broth.

Albóndigas Soup

Farmer's Stew Argentina

3 cups water
1 pound lean ground beef
2 tablespoons vegetable oil
1 medium onion, chopped
1 green bell pepper, cut into ½-inch pieces
1 red bell pepper, cut into ½-inch pieces
1 small sweet potato, peeled and cut into ½-inch pieces
1 large clove garlic, minced
1 tablespoon chopped fresh parsley
1 teaspoon salt
½ teaspoon granulated sugar
⅛ teaspoon ground cumin
3 cups beef broth, heated
½ pound zucchini, cut into ½-inch pieces
1 cup whole kernel corn
2 tablespoons raisins
1 teaspoon TABASCO® brand Pepper Sauce
1 small pear, firm but ripe, cut into 1-inch pieces
6 cups cooked white rice

Bring water to a boil in large saucepan. Remove saucepan from heat. Add ground beef, stirring to break meat into little pieces. Let stand 5 minutes, stirring once or twice, until most of the pink disappears from meat. Drain meat well, discarding water.

Heat oil in large deep skillet or Dutch oven over medium-high heat. Add onion and cook 4 to 5 minutes, stirring constantly, until limp and slightly brown. Add beef. Cook, stirring constantly, until all liquid has evaporated and meat is lightly browned, about 10 minutes.

Reduce heat to medium. Add bell peppers, sweet potato and garlic. Continue cooking and stirring 5 minutes, or until peppers and potatoes are slightly tender. Add parsley, salt, sugar and cumin. Stir and cook 1 minute to blend flavors. Pour beef broth into skillet. Add zucchini, corn, raisins and TABASCO® Sauce. Simmer gently 10 minutes, being careful not to boil. Add pear and simmer 10 additional minutes, or until all fruits and vegetables are tender. Ladle over rice in individual serving bowls. *Makes 6 servings*

Soups, Stews & Chilis

Hungarian Goulash Stew

¾ **pound lean ground beef (80% lean)**
½ **cup chopped onion**
1 **clove garlic, minced**
1 **package (4.8 ounces) PASTA RONI® Angel Hair Pasta with Herbs**
1 **can (14½ ounces) diced tomatoes, undrained**
1 **cup frozen corn *or* 1 can (8 ounces) whole kernel corn, drained**
1½ **teaspoons paprika**
⅛ **teaspoon black pepper**
   Sour cream (optional)

1. In 3-quart saucepan, brown ground beef, onion and garlic; drain.

2. Add 1⅓ cups water, pasta, Special Seasonings, tomatoes, frozen corn and seasonings. Bring just to a boil.

3. Reduce heat to medium.

4. Boil, uncovered, stirring frequently, 5 to 6 minutes or until pasta is tender.

5. Let stand 3 minutes or until desired consistency. Stir before serving. Serve with sour cream, if desired.   *Makes 4 servings*

Beefy Broccoli & Cheese Soup

  2 cups chicken broth
  1 package (10 ounces) frozen chopped broccoli, thawed
  ¼ cup chopped onion
  ¼ pound ground beef
  1 cup milk
  2 tablespoons all-purpose flour
  1 cup (4 ounces) shredded sharp Cheddar cheese
1½ teaspoons chopped fresh oregano *or* ½ teaspoon dried oregano
      leaves
    Salt and black pepper
    Hot pepper sauce

Bring broth to a boil in medium saucepan. Add broccoli and onion; cook 5 minutes or until broccoli is tender.

Meanwhile, brown ground beef in small skillet; drain. Gradually add milk to flour in small bowl, mixing until well blended. Add with ground beef to broth mixture; cook, stirring constantly, until mixture is thickened and bubbly.

Add cheese and oregano; stir until cheese is melted. Season with salt, pepper and hot pepper sauce to taste.   *Makes 4 to 5 servings*

Beefy Broccoli & Cheese Soup

30-Minute Chili Olé

1 cup chopped onion
2 cloves garlic, minced
1 tablespoon vegetable oil
2 pounds ground beef
1 (15-ounce) can tomato sauce
1 (14½-ounce) can stewed tomatoes
¾ cup A.1.® Steak Sauce
1 tablespoon chili powder
1 teaspoon ground cumin
1 (16-ounce) can black beans, rinsed and drained
1 (11-ounce) can corn, drained
    Shredded cheese, sour cream and chopped tomato, for garnish

Sauté onion and garlic in oil in 6-quart heavy pot over medium-high heat until tender.

Add beef; cook and stir until brown. Drain; stir in tomato sauce, stewed tomatoes, steak sauce, chili powder and cumin.

Heat to a boil; reduce heat to low. Cover; simmer for 10 minutes, stirring occasionally. Stir in beans and corn; simmer, uncovered, for 10 minutes.

Serve hot, garnished with cheese, sour cream and tomatoes.

Makes 8 servings

30-Minute Chili Olé

Texas Beef Stew

1 pound lean ground beef
1 small onion, chopped
1 can (28 ounces) crushed tomatoes with roasted garlic
1½ cups BIRDS EYE® frozen Farm Fresh Mixtures Broccoli,
      Cauliflower & Carrots
1 can (14½ ounces) whole new potatoes, halved
1 cup BIRDS EYE® frozen Sweet Corn
1 can (4½ ounces) chopped green chilies, drained
½ cup water

• In large saucepan, cook beef and onion over medium-high heat until beef is well browned, stirring occasionally.

• Stir in tomatoes, vegetables, potatoes with liquid, corn, chilies and water; bring to boil.

• Reduce heat to medium-low; cover and simmer 5 minutes or until heated through. *Makes 4 servings*

Serving Suggestion: Serve over rice and with warm crusty bread.

Tip: The smell of onions and garlic can penetrate into your cutting boards. Keep a separate cutting board exclusively for these vegetables.

Prep Time: 5 minutes
Cook Time: 15 minutes

Texas Beef Stew

Hearty Chili Mac

1 pound lean ground beef
1 can (14½ ounces) diced tomatoes, drained
1 cup chopped onion
1 clove garlic, minced
½ teaspoon salt
½ teaspoon ground cumin
½ teaspoon dried oregano leaves
¼ teaspoon black pepper
¼ teaspoon red pepper flakes
1 tablespoon chili powder
2 cups cooked macaroni

SLOW COOKER DIRECTIONS
Crumble ground beef into slow cooker. Add remaining ingredients, except macaroni, to slow cooker. Cover and cook on LOW 4 hours. Stir in cooked macaroni. Cover and cook on LOW 1 hour.

Makes 4 servings

Tip When preparing pasta to be used in a soup, casserole or slow cooker recipe, it's a good idea to reduce the cooking time by one-third. The pasta will continue to cook and absorb liquid in the final dish.

Hearty Chili Mac

Kansas City Steak Soup

Nonstick cooking spray
½ **pound ground sirloin or ground round beef**
1 **cup chopped onion**
3 **cups frozen mixed vegetables**
2 **cups water**
1 **can (14½ ounces) stewed tomatoes, undrained**
1 **cup sliced celery**
1 **beef bouillon cube**
½ **to 1 teaspoon black pepper**
1 **can (10½ ounces) defatted beef broth**
½ **cup all-purpose flour**

1. Spray Dutch oven with cooking spray. Heat over medium-high heat until hot. Add beef and onion. Cook and stir 5 minutes or until beef is browned.

2. Add vegetables, water, tomatoes with juice, celery, bouillon cube and pepper. Bring to a boil. Whisk together beef broth and flour until smooth; add to beef mixture, stirring constantly. Return mixture to a boil. Reduce heat to low. Cover and simmer 15 minutes, stirring frequently. *Makes 6 servings*

Note: If time permits, allow the soup to simmer an additional 30 minutes—the flavors just get better and better.

Kansas City Steak Soup

Spicy Quick and Easy Chili

    1 pound ground beef
    1 large clove garlic, minced
    1 can (15¼ ounces) DEL MONTE® Whole Kernel Golden Sweet Corn,
        drained
    1 can (16 ounces) kidney beans, drained
 1½ cups salsa, mild, medium or hot
    1 can (4 ounces) diced green chiles, undrained

1. Brown meat with garlic in large saucepan; drain.

2. Add remaining ingredients. Simmer, uncovered, 10 minutes,
stirring occasionally. Sprinkle with chopped green onions, if desired.

Makes 4 servings

Cheeseburger Macaroni Stew

    1 pound ground beef
    1 can (28 ounces) crushed tomatoes in puree
 1½ cups uncooked elbow macaroni
    2 tablespoons *French's®* Worcestershire Sauce
    1 cup shredded Cheddar cheese
 1½ cups *French's®* French Fried Onions

1. Cook meat in large nonstick skillet over medium-high heat until
browned and no longer pink; drain.

2. Add tomatoes, macaroni and *1½ cups water*. Bring to boiling.
Boil, partially covered, 10 minutes until macaroni is tender. Stir in
Worcestershire.

3. Sprinkle with cheese and French Fried Onions.

Makes 6 servings

Tip: For a Southwestern flavor, add 2 tablespoons chili powder to
ground beef and substitute 2 tablespoons *Frank's®* RedHot Sauce for
the Worcestershire.

Spicy Quick and Easy Chili

Taco Soup

Nonstick cooking spray
½ pound ground sirloin or ground round beef
1 cup chopped onion
1 can (16 ounces) pinto beans in Mexican-style sauce
1 can (about 14 ounces) no-salt-added stewed tomatoes, undrained
1 can (10 ounces) diced tomatoes and green chilies
2 teaspoons chili powder
5 (8-inch) corn tortillas
5 cups shredded iceberg lettuce
½ cup shredded sharp Cheddar cheese
¼ cup chopped fresh cilantro (optional)

1. Preheat oven to 350°F. Spray large saucepan with cooking spray. Heat over medium-high heat until hot. Add beef and onion. Cook and stir 6 minutes or until beef is browned. Add beans, stewed tomatoes with juice, diced tomatoes and green chilies and chili powder. Bring to a boil. Reduce heat to low. Cover and simmer 10 minutes.

2. Place tortillas on baking sheet. Spray tortillas lightly on both sides with cooking spray. Using pizza cutter, cut each tortilla into 6 wedges. Bake 5 minutes.

3. Divide lettuce equally among soup bowls. Ladle beef mixture over lettuce. Top with cheese and cilantro, if desired. Serve with tortilla wedges. *Makes 5 servings*

Prep and Cook Time: 25 minutes

Taco Soup

Wild Rice Soup

½ cup uncooked wild rice
1 pound lean ground beef
1 can (14½ ounces) chicken broth
1 can (10¾ ounces) condensed cream of mushroom soup
2 cups milk
1 cup (4 ounces) shredded Cheddar cheese
⅓ cup shredded carrot
1 package (.4 ounce) HIDDEN VALLEY® The Original Ranch®
    Buttermilk Recipe Salad Dressing Mix
Chopped green onions with tops

Cook rice according to package directions to make about 1½ cups cooked rice. In Dutch oven or large saucepan, brown beef; drain off excess fat. Stir in rice, chicken broth, cream of mushroom soup, milk, cheese, carrot and dry salad dressing mix. Heat to a simmer over low heat, stirring occasionally, about 15 minutes. Serve in warmed soup bowls; top with green onions. Garnish with additional green onions, if desired.   *Makes 6 to 8 servings*

Soups, Stews & Chilis

Minestrone Soup with Mini Meatballs

1 pound ground beef or ground turkey
1 teaspoon dried Italian seasoning
½ teaspoon garlic powder, divided
2 tablespoons vegetable oil, divided
5 cups assorted fresh vegetables*
1 envelope LIPTON® RECIPE SECRETS® Onion Soup Mix
4 cups water
1 can (28 ounces) Italian plum tomatoes, undrained
1 teaspoon sugar

Use any of the following to equal 5 cups: green beans, cut into 1-inch pieces; diced zucchini; diced carrot; or diced celery.

In medium bowl, combine ground beef, Italian seasoning and ¼ teaspoon garlic powder. Shape into 1-inch meatballs.

In 6-quart Dutch oven or heavy saucepan, heat 1 tablespoon oil over medium-high heat and brown meatballs. Remove meatballs. Heat remaining 1 tablespoon oil in same Dutch oven and cook vegetables, stirring frequently, 5 minutes or until crisp-tender. Stir in soup mix blended with water, remaining ¼ teaspoon garlic powder, tomatoes and sugar. Bring to a boil over high heat, breaking up tomatoes with wooden spoon. Reduce heat to low and simmer covered 25 minutes. Return meatballs to skillet. Continue simmering, covered, 5 minutes or until meatballs are heated through. Serve with grated Parmesan cheese and garlic bread, if desired.   *Makes 6 servings*

Soups, Stews & Chilis

Texas Chili

4 tablespoons vegetable oil, divided
2 large onions, chopped
3 large cloves garlic, minced
2 pounds boneless sirloin or round steak, cut into ½-inch cubes
1 pound ground beef
2 cans (16 ounces each) tomatoes in purée
1 can (15 to 19 ounces) red kidney beans, undrained
⅓ cup *Frank's® RedHot®* Cayenne Pepper Sauce
¼ cup chili powder
2 tablespoons ground cumin
1 tablespoon dried oregano leaves
½ teaspoon ground black pepper

1. Heat 1 tablespoon oil in 5-quart saucepan or Dutch oven. Add onions and garlic; cook 5 minutes or until tender. Transfer to small bowl; set aside.

2. Heat remaining 3 tablespoons oil in saucepan. Add sirloin and ground beef in batches; cook about 15 minutes or until well browned. Drain off fat.

3. Stir in remaining ingredients. Bring to a boil over medium-high heat. Return onions and garlic to saucepan. Simmer, partially covered, 1 hour or until meat is tender. Garnish with shredded Cheddar cheese and chopped green onion, if desired.   *Makes 10 servings*

Prep Time: 15 minutes
Cook Time: 1 hour 20 minutes

Texas Chili

Quick Beef Soup

1½ pounds lean ground beef
 1 cup chopped onion
 2 cloves garlic, finely chopped
 1 can (28 ounces) tomatoes, undrained
 6 cups water
 6 beef bouillon cubes
 ¼ teaspoon black pepper
1½ cups frozen peas, carrots and corn vegetable blend
 ½ cup uncooked orzo
    French bread (optional)

Cook beef, onion and garlic in large saucepan over medium-high heat until beef is brown, stirring to separate meat; drain fat.

Purée tomatoes with juice in covered blender or food processor. Add tomatoes with juice, water, bouillon cubes and pepper to meat mixture. Bring to a boil; reduce heat to low. Simmer, uncovered, 20 minutes. Add vegetables and orzo. Simmer 15 minutes more. Serve with French bread. *Makes 6 servings*

*Favorite recipe from **North Dakota Beef Commission***

Quick Beef Soup

Soups, Stews & Chilis

Chili with Chocolate

1 pound ground beef
1 medium onion, chopped
3 cloves garlic, minced, divided
1 can (28 ounces) diced tomatoes, undrained
1 can (15 ounces) chili beans
1½ tablespoons chili powder
1½ teaspoons cumin
1 tablespoon grated semisweet baking chocolate
Hot pepper sauce
Salt
Black pepper

SLOW COOKER DIRECTIONS

1. Brown ground beef, onion and 1 clove garlic in large nonstick skillet over medium-low heat. Drain off fat.

2. Place meat mixture in slow cooker. Add remaining ingredients, including 2 cloves garlic; mix well. Cover and cook on LOW 5 to 6 hours. Garnish as desired. *Makes 4 servings*

Tip

There's no need to peel cloves of garlic before putting them through a garlic press—the skins will stay behind in the press when the garlic cloves are forced through it.

Chili with Chocolate

Hearty Ground Beef Stew

1 pound ground beef
3 cloves garlic, minced
1 package (16 ounces) Italian-style frozen vegetables
2 cups Southern-style hash brown potatoes
1 jar (14 ounces) marinara sauce
1 can (10½ ounces) condensed beef broth
3 tablespoons *French's*® Worcestershire Sauce

Brown beef with garlic in large saucepan; drain. Add remaining ingredients. Heat to boiling. Cover. Reduce heat to medium-low. Cook 10 minutes or until vegetables are crisp-tender. Serve in warm bowls with garlic bread, if desired. *Makes 6 servings*

Quick & Easy Chili

1 pound ground beef
1 medium onion, chopped
2 cloves garlic, finely chopped
2 cans (15 ounces each) kidney, pinto or black beans, drained
1 jar (16 ounces) ORTEGA® SALSA (any flavor)
1 can (4 ounces) ORTEGA® Diced Green Chiles
2 teaspoons chili powder
½ teaspoon dried oregano, crushed
½ teaspoon ground cumin
   Topping suggestions: ORTEGA® SALSA, shredded Cheddar or Monterey Jack cheese, chopped tomatoes, sliced ripe olives, sliced green onions and sour cream

COOK beef, onion and garlic in large skillet over medium-high heat for 4 to 5 minutes or until beef is no longer pink; drain.

STIR in beans, salsa, chiles, chili powder, oregano and cumin. Bring to a boil. Reduce heat to low; cook, covered, for 20 to 25 minutes.

TOP as desired before serving. *Makes 6 servings*

Hearty Ground Beef Stew

Meaty Chili

1 pound coarsely ground beef
¼ pound ground Italian sausage
1 large onion, chopped
2 medium ribs celery, diced
2 fresh jalapeño peppers,* chopped
2 cloves garlic, minced
1 can (28 ounces) whole peeled tomatoes, undrained, cut up
1 can (15 ounces) pinto beans, drained
1 can (12 ounces) tomato juice
1 cup water
¼ cup ketchup
1 teaspoon sugar
1 teaspoon chili powder
½ teaspoon salt
½ teaspoon ground cumin
½ teaspoon dried thyme leaves
⅛ teaspoon black pepper

*Jalapeño peppers can sting and irritate the skin; wear rubber gloves when handling peppers and do not touch eyes. Wash hands after handling.

Cook beef, sausage, onion, celery, jalapeños and garlic in 5-quart Dutch oven over medium-high heat until meat is browned and onion is tender, stirring frequently.

Stir in tomatoes with juice, beans, tomato juice, water, ketchup, sugar, chili powder, salt, cumin, thyme and black pepper. Bring to a boil over high heat. Reduce heat to medium-low; simmer, uncovered, 30 minutes, stirring occasionally.

Ladle into bowls. Garnish, if desired.   *Makes 6 servings*

Meaty Chili

Riverboat Chili

2 pounds lean ground beef
2 large onions, chopped
1 large green pepper, chopped
2 cans (14½ ounces each) FRANK'S® or SNOWFLOSS® Original Style
    Diced Tomatoes, undrained
1 can (14½ ounces) FRANK'S® or SNOWFLOSS® Stewed Tomatoes,
    undrained
⅓ cup MISSISSIPPI® Barbecue Sauce
2 bay leaves
3 whole cloves
2 teaspoons chili powder
½ teaspoon cayenne pepper
½ teaspoon paprika
4 cans (15½ ounces each) dark red kidney beans

1. Brown ground beef in large stockpot. Drain grease.

2. Add onions, green pepper, diced tomatoes, stewed tomatoes, barbecue sauce, bay leaves, cloves, chili powder, cayenne pepper and paprika. Stir well.

3. Add kidney beans and stir well.

4. Cover and simmer 2 hours, stirring occasionally.

Makes 4 to 6 servings

Microwave Directions: Crumble beef into large casserole dish. Cook uncovered about 6 minutes, stirring at least twice to break up meat. Drain grease. Add onions, green pepper, diced tomatoes, stewed tomatoes, barbecue sauce, bay leaves, cloves, chili powder, cayenne pepper and paprika. Cook 1 minute. Stir well. Add kidney beans and stir well. Cover and cook 15 to 20 minutes, stirring occasionally. Cover and let stand 5 minutes.

Prep Time: 30 minutes
Cook Time: 2 hours

Mexican Vegetable Beef Soup

1 pound ground beef
½ cup chopped onion
1 package (1.0 ounce) LAWRY'S® Taco Spices & Seasonings
1 can (28 ounces) whole tomatoes, cut up
1 package (16 ounces) frozen mixed vegetables, thawed
1 can (15¼ ounces) kidney beans, undrained
1 can (14½ ounces) beef broth
  Corn chips
  Shredded cheddar cheese

In Dutch oven, brown ground beef and onion, stirring until beef is crumbly and onion is tender; drain fat. Add Taco Spices & Seasonings, tomatoes, vegetables, beans and broth. Bring to a boil over medium-high heat; reduce heat to low and cook, uncovered, 5 minutes, stirring occasionally. *Makes 6 servings*

Serving Suggestion: Top each serving with corn chips and shredded cheddar cheese.

Hint: For extra flavor, add chopped cilantro to beef mixture.

In a
FLASH

Beefy Bean & Walnut Stir-Fry

1 teaspoon vegetable oil
3 cloves garlic, minced
1 pound lean ground beef or ground turkey
1 bag (16 ounces) BIRDS EYE® frozen Cut Green Beans,
    thawed
1 teaspoon salt
½ cup walnut pieces

• In large skillet, heat oil and garlic over medium heat about 30 seconds.

• Add beef and beans; sprinkle with salt. Mix well.

• Cook 5 minutes or until beef is well browned, stirring occasionally.

• Stir in walnuts; cook 2 minutes more.

Makes 4 servings

Serving Suggestion: Serve over hot cooked egg noodles or rice.

Beefy Bean & Walnut Stir-Fry

Fast 'n Easy Chili

1½ pounds ground beef
  1 envelope LIPTON® RECIPE SECRETS® Onion Soup Mix*
  1 can (15 to 19 ounces) red kidney or black beans, drained
1½ cups water
  1 can (8 ounces) tomato sauce
  4 teaspoons chili powder

*Also terrific with LIPTON® RECIPE SECRETS® Beefy Mushroom, Onion-Mushroom or Beefy Onion Soup Mix.

1. In 12-inch skillet, brown ground beef over medium-high heat; drain.

2. Stir in remaining ingredients. Bring to a boil over high heat. Reduce heat to low and simmer covered, stirring occasionally, 20 minutes. Serve, if desired, over hot cooked rice.

Makes 6 servings

First Alarm Chili: Add 5 teaspoons chili powder.

Second Alarm Chili: Add 2 tablespoons chili powder.

Third Alarm Chili: Add chili powder at your own risk.

Fast 'n Easy Chili

Velveeta® Cheesy Tacos

1 pound ground beef
¼ cup water
1 package (1¼ ounces) TACO BELL® HOME ORIGINALS®* Taco
    Seasoning Mix
¾ pound (12 ounces) VELVEETA® Mexican Pasteurized Process
    Cheese Spread with Jalapeño Peppers, cut up
1 package (4.5 ounces) TACO BELL® HOME ORIGINALS®* Taco Shells
    or 12 flour tortillas (8 inch)

*TACO BELL and HOME ORIGINALS are registered trademarks owned and licensed
by Taco Bell Corp.

1. Brown meat in large skillet; drain. Stir in water and taco
seasoning mix.

2. Add VELVEETA; stir on low heat until VELVEETA is melted.

3. Fill heated taco shells with meat mixture. Top with your favorite
toppings, such as shredded lettuce, chopped tomato and Taco Bell
Home Originals Thick 'N Chunky Salsa.   *Makes 4 to 6 servings*

Serving Suggestion: Cheesy Tacos are a fun family dinner. Have your
child place the family's favorite taco toppings, such as shredded
lettuce and chopped tomato, in a muffin tin to pass around at the
table.

Prep Time: 5 minutes
Cook Time: 15 minutes

Velveeta® Cheesy Tacos

Polynesian Burgers

¼ cup LAWRY'S® Teriyaki Marinade with Pineapple Juice
1 pound ground beef
½ cup chopped green bell pepper
4 onion-flavored hamburger buns
1 can (5¼ ounces) pineapple slices, drained
Lettuce leaves

In medium bowl, combine Teriyaki Marinade, ground beef and bell pepper; mix well. Let stand 10 to 15 minutes. Shape into 4 patties. Grill or broil burgers 8 to 10 minutes or until desired doneness, turning halfway through grilling time. Serve burgers on onion buns topped with pineapple slices and lettuce.   *Makes 4 servings*

Serving Suggestion: Serve with assorted fresh fruits.

Hint: For extra teriyaki flavor, brush buns and pineapple slices with additional Teriyaki Marinade; grill or broil until buns are lightly toasted and pineapple is heated through.

Taco Taters

1 pound ground beef
1 jar (26 to 28 ounces) RAGÚ® Old World Style® Pasta Sauce
1 package (1.25 ounces) taco seasoning mix
6 large all-purpose potatoes, unpeeled and baked

1. In 12-inch skillet, brown ground beef over medium-high heat; drain. Stir in Ragú Pasta Sauce and taco seasoning mix and cook 5 minutes.

2. To serve, cut a lengthwise slice from top of each potato. Evenly spoon beef mixture onto each potato. Garnish, if desired, with shredded Cheddar cheese and sour cream.   *Makes 6 servings*

Prep Time: 5 minutes
Cook Time: 15 minutes

Polynesian Burger

Crunchy Layered Beef & Bean Salad

1 pound ground beef or turkey
2 cans (15 to 19 ounces *each*) black beans or pinto beans, rinsed and drained
1 can (14½ ounces) stewed tomatoes, undrained
1⅓ cups *French's®* French Fried Onions, divided
1 tablespoon *Frank's®* RedHot® Cayenne Pepper Sauce
1 package (1¼ ounces) taco seasoning mix
6 cups shredded lettuce
1 cup (4 ounces) shredded Cheddar or Monterey Jack cheese

1. Cook beef in large nonstick skillet over medium heat until thoroughly browned; drain well. Stir in beans, tomatoes, ⅔ *cup* French Fried Onions, **Frank's RedHot** Sauce and taco seasoning. Heat to boiling. Cook over medium heat 5 minutes, stirring occasionally.

2. Spoon beef mixture over lettuce on serving platter. Top with cheese.

3. Microwave remaining ⅔ *cup* onions 1 minute on HIGH. Sprinkle over salad. *Makes 6 servings*

Prep Time: 10 minutes
Cook Time: 6 minutes

Crunchy Layered Beef & Bean Salad

Quick Chunky Chili

1 pound lean ground beef
1 medium onion, chopped
1 tablespoon chili powder
1½ teaspoons ground cumin
2 cans (16 ounces each) diced tomatoes, undrained
1 can (15 ounces) pinto beans, drained
½ cup prepared salsa
½ cup (2 ounces) shredded Cheddar cheese
3 tablespoons sour cream
4 teaspoons sliced black olives

Combine meat and onion in 3-quart saucepan; cook over high heat until meat is no longer pink, breaking meat apart with wooden spoon. Add chili powder and cumin; stir 1 minute or until fragrant. Add tomatoes, beans and salsa. Bring to a boil; stir constantly. Reduce heat to low, simmer, covered, 10 minutes. Ladle into bowls. Top with cheese, sour cream and olives.   *Makes 4 (1½-cup) servings*

Serving Suggestion: Serve with tossed green salad and cornbread muffins.

Prep and Cook Time: 25 minutes

Quick Chunky Chili

Ranchero Onion Burgers

  1 pound ground beef
  ½ cup salsa
  ½ cup (2 ounces) shredded Monterey Jack cheese
1⅓ cups *French's®* French Fried Onions, divided
  ½ teaspoon garlic powder
  ¼ teaspoon ground black pepper
  4 hamburger rolls

Combine beef, salsa, cheese, ⅔ *cup* French Fried Onions, garlic powder and pepper in large bowl. Shape into 4 patties.

Place patties on oiled grid. Grill* over medium coals 10 minutes or until no longer pink in center, turning once. Serve on rolls. Garnish with additional salsa, if desired. Top with remaining ⅔ *cup* onions.

Makes 4 servings

*Or, broil 6 inches from heat.

Tip: For extra-crispy warm onion flavor, heat French Fried Onions in the microwave for 1 minute. Or, place in foil pan and heat on the grill 2 minutes.

Prep Time: 10 minutes
Cook Time: 10 minutes

Ranchero Onion Burger

Salisbury Steaks with Mushroom-Wine Sauce

1 pound lean ground beef sirloin
¾ teaspoon garlic salt or seasoned salt
¼ teaspoon black pepper
2 tablespoons butter or margarine
1 package (8 ounces) sliced button mushrooms *or* 2 packages
    (4 ounces each) sliced exotic mushrooms
2 tablespoons sweet vermouth or ruby port wine
1 jar (12 ounces) *or* 1 can (10½ ounces) beef gravy

1. Heat large heavy nonstick skillet over medium-high heat 3 minutes or until hot.* Meanwhile, combine ground sirloin, garlic salt and pepper; mix well. Shape mixture into four ¼-inch-thick oval patties.

2. Place patties in skillet as they are formed; cook 3 minutes per side or until browned. Transfer to plate. Pour off drippings.

3. Melt butter in skillet; add mushrooms. Cook and stir 2 minutes. Add vermouth; cook 1 minute. Add gravy; mix well.

4. Return patties to skillet; simmer uncovered over medium heat 2 minutes for medium or until desired doneness, turning meat and stirring sauce. *Makes 4 servings*

If pan is not heavy, use medium heat.

Note: For a special touch, sprinkle steaks with chopped parsley or chives.

Prep and Cook Time: 20 minutes

Salisbury Steak with
Mushroom-Wine Sauce

Groovy Angel Hair Goulash

1 pound lean ground beef
2 tablespoons margarine or butter
1 (4.8-ounce) package PASTA RONI® Angel Hair Pasta with Herbs
1 (14½-ounce) can diced tomatoes, undrained
1 cup frozen or canned corn, drained

1. In large skillet over medium-high heat, brown ground beef. Remove from skillet; drain. Set aside.

2. In same skillet, bring 1½ cups water and margarine to a boil.

3. Stir in pasta; cook 1 minute or just until pasta softens slightly. Stir in tomatoes, corn, beef and Special Seasonings; return to a boil. Reduce heat to medium. Gently boil uncovered, 4 to 5 minutes or until pasta is tender, stirring frequently. Let stand 3 to 5 minutes before serving. *Makes 4 servings*

Prep Time: 5 minutes
Cook Time: 15 minutes

Monterey Black Bean Tortilla Supper

1 pound ground beef, browned and drained
1½ cups bottled salsa
1 (15-ounce) can black beans, drained
4 (8-inch) flour tortillas
2 cups (8 ounces) shredded Wisconsin Monterey Jack cheese*

*For authentic Mexican flavor, substitute 2 cups shredded Wisconsin Queso Blanco.

Heat oven to 400°F. Combine ground beef, salsa and beans. In lightly greased 2-quart round casserole, layer one tortilla, ⅔ cup meat mixture and ½ cup cheese. Repeat layers three times. Bake 30 minutes or until heated through. *Makes 5 to 6 servings*

*Favorite recipe from **Wisconsin Milk Marketing Board***

Nacho Bacho

1½ pounds ground beef
1 cup chunky hot salsa
½ cup salad dressing
2 tablespoons Italian seasoning
1 tablespoon chili powder
2 cups (8 ounces) shredded Colby-Jack cheese, divided
3 cups nacho-flavored tortilla chips, crushed
1 cup sour cream
½ cup sliced black olives

Brown ground beef; drain. In medium bowl, combine salsa, salad dressing, Italian seasoning and chili powder. Add beef. Place in 11×7-inch baking dish. Top with 1 cup cheese. Cover with crushed chips and remaining cheese. Bake at 350°F 20 minutes. Garnish with sour cream and sliced olives. *Makes 4 servings*

Favorite recipe from **North Dakota Beef Commission**

Creamy Beef and Vegetable Casserole

1 pound lean ground beef
1 small onion, chopped
1 bag (16 ounces) BIRDS EYE® frozen Farm Fresh Mixtures Broccoli, Corn & Red Peppers
1 can (10¾ ounces) cream of mushroom soup

• In medium skillet, brown beef and onion; drain excess fat.

• Meanwhile, in large saucepan, cook vegetables according to package directions; drain.

• Stir in beef mixture and soup. Cook over medium heat until heated through. *Makes 4 servings*

Serving Suggestion: Serve over rice and sprinkle with ½ cup shredded Cheddar cheese.

Speedy Beef & Bean Burritos

8 flour tortillas (7-inch)
1 pound ground beef
1 cup chopped onion
1 teaspoon minced garlic
1 can (15 ounces) black beans, drained and rinsed
1 cup spicy thick and chunky salsa
2 teaspoons ground cumin
1 bunch cilantro
2 cups (8 ounces) shredded cojack or Monterey Jack cheese

1. Wrap tortillas in foil; place on center rack in oven. Heat oven to 350°F; heat tortillas 15 minutes.

2. While tortillas are warming, prepare burrito filling. Combine beef, onion and garlic in large skillet; cook over medium-high heat until beef is no longer pink, breaking beef apart with wooden spoon. Pour off drippings.

3. Stir beans, salsa and cumin into beef mixture; reduce heat to medium. Cover and simmer 10 minutes, stirring once.

4. While filling is simmering, chop enough cilantro to measure ¼ cup. Stir into filling. Spoon filling down centers of warm tortillas; top with cheese. Roll up and serve immediately.   *Makes 4 servings*

Prep and Cook Time: 20 minutes

Speedy Beef & Bean Burritos

Joe's Special

1 pound lean ground beef
2 cups sliced mushrooms
1 small onion, chopped
2 teaspoons Worcestershire sauce
1 teaspoon dried oregano leaves
1 teaspoon ground nutmeg
½ teaspoon garlic powder
½ teaspoon salt
1 package (10 ounces) frozen chopped spinach, thawed
4 large eggs, lightly beaten
⅓ cup grated Parmesan cheese

1. Spray large skillet with nonstick cooking spray. Add ground beef, mushrooms and onion; cook over medium-high heat 6 to 8 minutes or until onion is tender, breaking beef apart with wooden spoon. Add Worcestershire, oregano, nutmeg, garlic powder and salt. Cook until meat is no longer pink.

2. Drain spinach (do not squeeze dry); stir into meat mixture. Push mixture to one side of pan. Reduce heat to medium. Pour eggs into other side of pan; cook, without stirring, 1 to 2 minutes or until set on bottom. Lift eggs to allow uncooked portion to flow underneath. Repeat until softly set. Gently stir into meat mixture and heat through. Stir in cheese. *Makes 4 to 6 servings*

Serving Suggestion: Serve with salsa and toast.

Prep and Cook Time: 20 minutes

Joe's Special

Mini Mexican Burger Bites

1½ **pounds ground beef**
½ **cup finely chopped red, yellow or green bell pepper**
2 **tablespoons** *French's*® **Worcestershire Sauce**
1 **teaspoon** *Frank's*® *RedHot*® **Cayenne Pepper Sauce**
1 **teaspoon dried oregano leaves**
¼ **teaspoon salt**
12 **mini dinner rolls**
   Shredded Cheddar cheese

1. Gently combine all ingredients except rolls and cheese in large bowl. Shape into 12 mini patties. Broil or grill patties 4 to 6 minutes for medium doneness (160°F internal temperature), turning once.

2. Arrange burgers on rolls and top with Cheddar cheese. Top with shredded lettuce if desired. *Makes 6 servings*

Prep Time: 5 minutes
Cook Time: 8 minutes

Western Hash

1 **pound ground beef**
1 **can (28 ounces) tomatoes, undrained**
1 **cup long grain rice, uncooked**
1 **cup chopped green pepper**
½ **cup chopped onion**
½ **pound (8 ounces) VELVEETA® Pasteurized Prepared Cheese Product, sliced**

1. Brown meat in large skillet on medium-high heat; drain.

2. Add tomatoes, rice, green pepper and onion; cover. Reduce heat to medium-low; simmer 25 minutes.

3. Top with VELVEETA; continue cooking until VELVEETA is melted.
Makes 6 servings

Mini Mexican Burger Bites

BBQ Beef Pizza

½ **pound lean ground beef**
¾ **cup prepared barbecue sauce**
 1 **medium green bell pepper**
 1 **(14-inch) prepared pizza crust**
 3 **to 4 onion slices, separated into rings**
½ **(2¼-ounce can) sliced black olives, drained**
 1 **cup (4 ounces) shredded cheese (Colby and Monterey Jack mix)**

1. Preheat oven to 400°F. Place meat in large skillet; cook over high heat 6 to 8 minutes or until meat is no longer pink, breaking meat apart with wooden spoon. Pour off drippings; remove from heat. Stir in barbecue sauce.

2. While meat is cooking, seed bell pepper and slice into ¼-inch-thick rings. Place pizza crust on baking pan. Spread meat mixture over pizza crust to within ½ inch of edge. Arrange onion slices and pepper rings over meat. Sprinkle with olives and cheese. Bake 8 minutes or until cheese is melted. Cut into 8 wedges. *Makes 3 to 4 servings*

Prep and Cook Time: 20 minutes

BBQ Beef Pizza

Burrito Burgers

6 tablespoons A.1.® Original or A.1.® BOLD & SPICY Steak Sauce, divided
1 (4-ounce) can diced green chiles, divided
3 tablespoons dairy sour cream
1 pound ground beef
4 (6½-inch) flour tortillas
1 medium tomato, sliced
1 cup shredded lettuce
½ cup shredded Cheddar cheese (2 ounces)

Blend 2 tablespoons steak sauce, 2 tablespoons chiles and sour cream. Cover; refrigerate until ready to serve.

Mix beef, remaining ¼ cup steak sauce and chiles. Shape mixture into 4 (4-inch) oval patties. Grill burgers over medium heat or broil 6 inches from heat source 5 minutes on each side or until beef is no longer pink in center. Place each burger in center of 1 tortilla; top evenly with tomato, lettuce, cheese and chilled sauce. Fold edges of tortillas in like a burrito. Serve immediately.   *Makes 4 servings*

Tip

To warm tortillas before using them, wrap a stack of tortillas in foil and place in a 350°F oven for 10 to 15 minutes. (If you're grilling the burgers, place the foil-wrapped stack of tortillas near the outer edge of the grill.)

Burrito Burger

Sweet and Sour Beef

1 pound lean ground beef
1 small onion, thinly sliced
2 teaspoons minced fresh ginger
1 package (16 ounces) frozen mixed vegetables (snap peas, carrots,
   water chestnuts, pineapple, red pepper)
6 to 8 tablespoons bottled sweet and sour sauce or sauce from
   vegetable mix
Cooked rice

1. Place meat, onion and ginger in large skillet; cook over high heat 6 to 8 minutes or until no longer pink, breaking apart with wooden spoon. Pour off drippings.

2. Stir in frozen vegetables and sauce. Cook, covered, 6 to 8 minutes, stirring every 2 minutes or until vegetables are heated through. Serve over rice.   *Makes 4 servings*

Serving Suggestion: Serve with sliced Asian apple-pears.

Prep and Cook Time: 15 minutes

Sweet and Sour Beef

Velveeta® Salsa Mac

1 pound ground beef
1 jar (16 ounces) TACO BELL® HOME ORIGINALS®* Thick 'N Chunky Salsa
1¾ cups water
2 cups (8 ounces) elbow macaroni, uncooked
¾ pound (12 ounces) VELVEETA® Pasteurized Prepared Cheese Product, cut up

*TACO BELL and HOME ORIGINALS are registered trademarks owned and licensed by Taco Bell Corp.

1. Brown meat in large skillet; drain.

2. Stir in salsa and water. Bring to boil. Stir in macaroni. Reduce heat to medium-low; cover. Simmer 8 to 10 minutes or until macaroni is tender.

3. Add VELVEETA; stir until melted.   *Makes 4 to 6 servings*

Spicy Substitute: For an extra spicy kick in Salsa Mac, try making it with VELVEETA Mild or Hot Mexican Pasteurized Process Cheese Spread with Jalapeño Peppers. Be careful though...the hot is really hot!

Prep Time: 10 minutes
Cook Time: 15 minutes

Velveeta® Salsa Mac

French Bread Pizza

½ **pound bulk Italian turkey sausage**
½ **pound extra lean ground beef**
1 **can (15.5 ounces) HUNT'S® Manwich Sloppy Joe Sauce**
2 **tablespoons TREASURE CAVE® Shredded Parmesan Cheese**
1 **teaspoon dried oregano**
1 **loaf (16 ounces) unsliced French bread**
1 **cup shredded fat-free mozzarella cheese**

1. In large skillet, brown sausage with beef; drain. Stir in Manwich Sauce, Parmesan cheese and oregano. Simmer, uncovered, for 5 minutes.

2. Halve bread lengthwise. Top *each* half loaf with *half* of meat mixture and mozzarella cheese.

3. Place on baking sheet and broil 5 to 6 inches from heat source for 3 minutes or until hot and bubbly. Cut into 16 slices.

Makes 16 servings

Tacos Olé

1 **pound ground beef or turkey**
1 **cup salsa**
¼ **cup *Frank's® RedHot® Cayenne Pepper Sauce***
2 **teaspoons chili powder**
8 **taco shells, heated**
   Garnish: chopped tomatoes, shredded lettuce, sliced olives, sour cream, shredded cheese

1. Cook beef in skillet over medium-high heat 5 minutes or until browned, stirring to separate meat; drain. Stir in salsa, ***Frank's RedHot*** Sauce and chili powder. Heat to boiling. Reduce heat to medium-low. Cook 5 minutes, stirring often.

2. To serve, spoon meat mixture into taco shells. Splash on more ***Frank's RedHot*** Sauce to taste. Garnish as desired.

Makes 4 servings

In a Flash

Spanish Skillet Supper

½ **pound ground beef**
1 **small onion, chopped**
2¼ **cups water**
  1 **cup frozen whole kernel corn, partially thawed**
  1 **tablespoon margarine or butter**
  1 **package LIPTON® Rice & Sauce—Spanish**
  ¼ **cup shredded Cheddar cheese (about 1 ounce) (optional)**

1. Brown ground beef and onion in 12-inch nonstick skillet over medium-high heat; drain. Remove and set aside.

2. Add water, corn, margarine and Rice & Sauce—Spanish and bring to a boil. Continue boiling over medium heat, stirring occasionally, 10 minutes or until rice is tender.

3. Stir in beef mixture; heat through. Sprinkle with cheese.

Makes about 2 servings

Corny Sloppy Joes

1 **pound lean ground beef or ground turkey**
1 **small onion, chopped**
1 **can (15½ ounces) sloppy joe sauce**
1 **box (10 ounces) BIRDS EYE® frozen Sweet Corn**
6 **hamburger buns**

• In large skillet, cook beef and onion over high heat until beef is well browned.

• Stir in sloppy joe sauce and corn; reduce heat to low and simmer 5 minutes or until heated through.

• Serve mixture in hamburger buns. *Makes 6 servings*

Serving Suggestion: Sprinkle with shredded Cheddar cheese.

*The publisher would like to thank
the companies and organizations listed below
for the use of their recipes and photographs in this publication.*

A.1.® Steak Sauce
Barilla America, Inc.
Birds Eye®
ConAgra Foods®
Del Monte Corporation
The Fremont Company, Makers of Frank's & SnowFloss Kraut
and Tomato Products
The Golden Grain Company®
Grey Poupon® Dijon Mustard
The Hidden Valley® Food Products Company
Kraft Foods Holdings
Lawry's® Foods, Inc.
McIlhenny Company (TABASCO® brand Pepper Sauce)
Nestlé USA
North Dakota Beef Commission
North Dakota Wheat Commission
The Quaker® Oatmeal Kitchens
Reckitt Benckiser
Riviana Foods Inc.
The J.M. Smucker Company
Uncle Ben's Inc.
Unilever Bestfoods North America
USA Dry Pea & Lentil Council
Wisconsin Milk Marketing Board

220

Index

METRIC CONVERSION CHART

VOLUME MEASUREMENTS (dry)

$^1/_8$ teaspoon = 0.5 mL
$^1/_4$ teaspoon = 1 mL
$^1/_2$ teaspoon = 2 mL
$^3/_4$ teaspoon = 4 mL
1 teaspoon = 5 mL
1 tablespoon = 15 mL
2 tablespoons = 30 mL
$^1/_4$ cup = 60 mL
$^1/_3$ cup = 75 mL
$^1/_2$ cup = 125 mL
$^2/_3$ cup = 150 mL
$^3/_4$ cup = 175 mL
1 cup = 250 mL
2 cups = 1 pint = 500 mL
3 cups = 750 mL
4 cups = 1 quart = 1 L

VOLUME MEASUREMENTS (fluid)

1 fluid ounce (2 tablespoons) = 30 mL
4 fluid ounces ($^1/_2$ cup) = 125 mL
8 fluid ounces (1 cup) = 250 mL
12 fluid ounces (1$^1/_2$ cups) = 375 mL
16 fluid ounces (2 cups) = 500 mL

WEIGHTS (mass)

$^1/_2$ ounce = 15 g
1 ounce = 30 g
3 ounces = 90 g
4 ounces = 120 g
8 ounces = 225 g
10 ounces = 285 g
12 ounces = 360 g
16 ounces = 1 pound = 450 g

DIMENSIONS

$^1/_{16}$ inch = 2 mm
$^1/_8$ inch = 3 mm
$^1/_4$ inch = 6 mm
$^1/_2$ inch = 1.5 cm
$^3/_4$ inch = 2 cm
1 inch = 2.5 cm

OVEN TEMPERATURES

250°F = 120°C
275°F = 140°C
300°F = 150°C
325°F = 160°C
350°F = 180°C
375°F = 190°C
400°F = 200°C
425°F = 220°C
450°F = 230°C

BAKING PAN SIZES

Utensil	Size in Inches/Quarts	Metric Volume	Size in Centimeters
Baking or Cake Pan (square or rectangular)	8×8×2	2 L	20×20×5
	9×9×2	2.5 L	23×23×5
	12×8×2	3 L	30×20×5
	13×9×2	3.5 L	33×23×5
Loaf Pan	8×4×3	1.5 L	20×10×7
	9×5×3	2 L	23×13×7
Round Layer Cake Pan	8×1½	1.2 L	20×4
	9×1½	1.5 L	23×4
Pie Plate	8×1¼	750 mL	20×3
	9×1¼	1 L	23×3
Baking Dish or Casserole	1 quart	1 L	—
	1½ quart	1.5 L	—
	2 quart	2 L	—